Table of contents:

About the Author

Steven Herrick is the author of twenty-one books for children and young adults. In Australia, his books have won the New South Wales Premier's Literary Award in 2000 and 2005 and the Western Australia Premier's Literary Award in 2013. His books have also been shortlisted for the prestigious Children's Book Council of Australia Book of the Year Awards on seven occasions. He is published in the USA by Simon and Schuster and Boyds Mill Press. He has also been published in the UK and The Netherlands.

Steven has written travel articles, features and restaurant reviews for newspapers and magazines and regularly travels the world performing his poetry and conducting author talks in schools. He lives in the Blue Mountains in Australia with his wife Cathie, a belly dance teacher. They have two adult sons, Jack and Joe.

This is his fourth travel book, following on from the successful *'baguettes and bicycles,' 'bordeaux and bicycles.'* and *'bratwurst and bicycles.'*

www.stevenherrick.com.au

dothebikething.blogspot.com.au

cycling to Bohemia

by

Steven Herrick

Eurovelo Series Book One: *'baguettes and bicycles'* published
by
Amazon and CreateSpace in 2012.
Eurovelo Series Book Two: *'bordeaux and bicycles'* published
by
Amazon and CreateSpace in 2013.
Eurovelo Series Book Three: *'bratwurst and bicycles'* published
by
Amazon and CreateSpace in 2014.

Dedicated to Jean-Paul and Regine

at Le Petit Plessis.

Wise and welcoming guardians of Craig and Jenny.

Introduction

It's the last day of summer in St Malo, France. A throng of holiday makers promenade along the beachfront. On the sand, a man in a red shirt and cut-off jeans digs a large hole while his wife and son sleep on a towel. A dozen teenagers play beach soccer, their discarded shirts used as goal posts. An old man in a towelling hat licks an ice-cream cone while walking his dog.

My wife, Cathie and I wheel our bicycles, nicknamed Jenny and Craig through the crowd. We rest them against the rock wall and gaze out to sea. A trickle of sweat runs down my back. Tomorrow, on the first day of autumn we will begin a bicycle journey from here in the most ancient of Breton towns to Prague in the Czech Republic.

If you ask Google, it'll plot a relatively straight line across Europe for just over one thousand kilometres. However, we won't be taking that route of highways, industry and nameless forests.

We plan to follow the Euro Velo 4 cycle route which snakes along the Brittany and Normandy coastline of France before crossing into Belgium. From there we'll enter the most cycle-friendly of all countries, The Netherlands and plot a rather haphazard course across the lowlands before linking with the mighty Rhine river leading us through Germany. After arriving in the river town of Mainz we'll turn left and follow the Main tributary to its source in the Fichtelgebirge Mountains near the border. Finally, we'll cross into the Czech Republic and follow the path all the way to the capital of Bohemia, the magical city of Prague.

Rivers are notorious for taking their time, for curling and twisting back on themselves and leading the weary traveller on a fine dance. A river, unless in flood, does not understand a straight line. As compensation for all the extra kilometres, most of the cycling will be along flat lands.

'How long did you say it was,' Cathie asks.

'Two thousand five hundred kilometres,' I answer, watching a ferry head slowly out to sea.

'I've never ridden that far before,' she says.

'Me neither.'

Cathie reaches for my hand. 'I'll need lots of food for fuel.'

We both smile. My wife coined the phrase, *cycling is just an interlude between meals.*

Cycling is about the simple pleasures of travel - the landscape, food and wine, the people and the joy of never rushing. The world passes at a leisurely pace. The day is measured not by how many kilometres we cycle, but by the people we meet, the meals we consume and the sights and smells that can only be fully appreciated at fifteen kilometres per hour. While Richard Branson plots a way to get tourists into outer-space at an astronomical cost to both the customer and the planet, we plan to tread lightly across the continent on two creaky old bicycles.

St Malo is a fortified island on a prominent headland, former home to pirates and profiteers. We lock Craig and Jenny against a pole and enter under the archway. The profiteers remain, now dressed in the black and white of a hundred waiters all vying for the tourist traffic ambling past their seafood restaurants. A procession of blackboard menus promise moules and frites at ten euros per serve, accompanied by a bowl of local cider. It's tempting but instead we choose the healthier pursuit of a stroll along the ramparts. It's a glorious blue sky day with a gentle breeze blowing across the channel from Cornwall. On a west-facing beach below the great wall, hundreds of sunbathers frolic on the sand. Teenage boys daredevil from a diving board, splashing into an ocean pool. They cast eager glances at the circle of girls on beach towels nearby. We admire the cobblestone narrow lanes of the old fort town from this vantage point on the rampart.

At the end of the wall, we descend into the late afternoon seeking kouign-amann and coffee. The Breton pastry has heart-attack levels of butter and sugar and is one of my favourite French cakes. With such a high demand, many of the shops sell them reheated from a microwave. I don't know much about French pastries, but an irradiated one is not to my liking. We retreat into the Cafe de Coin, a watering hole that bills itself as *Etablissement classe Cafe Hysterique et Patrimone Intergalactique*. We order two noisette coffees and spend an hour admiring this free museum of toys from times past, with an emphasis, as the sign suggests, on the toy tin rocket ships of every young boy's dream. It's a lovely quiet place run by an eccentric old man who stands proudly at the counter witnessing the joy on the faces of his customers.

'How long do you think this weather will hold,' I say.

Cathie stirs her coffee and smiles, 'Until eight o'clock tomorrow morning.'

'Don't be so negative,' I say.

Cathie leans forward, 'I hereby predict it won't rain for the next week. Nothing but blue skies.'

'That's better,' I say.

She opens her iPad which shows the weather forecast. Not a rain cloud in sight.

We wander back to Craig and Jenny and slowly cruise along the waterfront. The breeze has increased. The wind-surfing buggies spear across the sand at a frightening pace. A crowd gathers to watch the cannonball run.

Back at our hotel, we sit in the sun-drenched main square of Parame, a small village on the outskirts of St Malo. I order a beer and Cathie a Ricard. We are the only customers. The hotel used to be a family home dating from 1930. Our room overlooks the square and is decorated with cream and maroon striped wallpaper, regal high-backed chairs and enough brocade to satisfy any Frenchman.

Craig and Jenny rest in the shade of a tree.

'To Bohemia,' I say.

We clink our glasses and watch the sun set over the stone buildings of the main street. Tomorrow we cycle east.

Chapter One:

Brittany, France

After a fine breakfast, Cathie and I eagerly load our panniers onto Craig and Jenny and ease ourselves into the strong morning light. We cruise downhill to the promenade and a cool breeze sweeps us up our first hill of the day. Craig and Jenny crest the slight incline with ease. The suburbs of St Malo follow the rugged coastline for a few kilometres before opening out into cabbage fields tilting down to the bay.

I'm very excited to be underway and constantly have to remind Craig to slow down and enjoy the view. Perhaps a year spent in a dusty French barn has made my hybrid red bicycle eager to appreciate the outdoors?

On the road ahead a single racing cyclist, kitted out in green and white with a peaked cap, crests a hill and silently glides towards us. We nod good morning as he races past.

At the Harve de Rotheneuf, we stop to look across the bay. Fishing boats lie in wayward grace at low tide as oyster catchers and egrets daintily parade on the mud. A fisherman wheels his dinghy down to the hard sand. He has wavy blond hair, wears shorts and a t-shirt and can't help but smile at the day ahead of him. On a morning as bright and clear as this perhaps it's not whether you catch a fish but how long you can stay away from the office. The haven was named after a family of pirates. It's a peaceful shelter to drink rum and count ill-gotten gains.

The road meanders up and down and we have it all to ourselves, save for the occasional delivery van. On a long stretch of beach, a group of walkers struggle through the sand. They each carry walking poles and a backpack full of provisions for their day ahead. On an island just offshore, a stone double-storey house looks back to the mainland. As I crest the next rise, I see the distant fortress of Mont Saint-Michel in the haze of the Channel. It appears so close and yet we have fifty kilometres of shoreline to navigate before reaching one of the most visited places in France.

After another high speed downhill, we arrive in Cancale which trumpets itself as the oyster capital of the world. The oysters from this area have been prized for two thousand years and were eaten by the soldiers of Julius Caesar and delivered daily to Louis the Fourteenth. While the vast majority are farmed in oyster parks, some are still harvested from the bay.

Cue twenty seafood restaurants along the crowded port. It's only 10am and yet scores of tourists are already perusing the menus. Now I enjoy a feast as much as the next glutton, but rarely am I so focused on food as to be scanning the possibilities two hours before dining. Cancale is justly famous for oysters but perhaps some physical activity like walking around the bay would increase an appetite?

We cycle up a hill and are rewarded with a lovely view back down to Cancale. The row of stone houses gaze out to the fishing boats moored at anchor. The white-hulled boats tilt and bob on the tide.

Incongruously, we spy two kangaroos in a paddock along the D76. I stop to rub my eyes. A kangaroo in Brittany? Kangaroos are notoriously flighty animals. They do not make suitable pets and yet some misguided local has fenced them into a green field, thousands of miles from their natural habitat in the vast Australian plains. I sigh and wonder at the future for these noble animals.

Along the back roads are numerous dark wooden shacks used for grading oysters. They are distinctly ramshackle and smell strongly of the ocean. Next to the shacks are tangled fishing nets and upturned dinghies. We follow the bay until the village of Cherrueix hoping to find a restaurant for lunch. Alas, the beachfront establishment is closed for the season. A tabac offers sandwiches and coffee, but on our first day we want something more indicative of the region. We buy a chocolate bar to ward off hunger and continue along a beautiful voie verte - or green way - for thirteen kilometres beside carrot, corn and leek fields. A sign announces the European Union has invested one million euros on the gravel bike path. Well done EU! It's very quiet atop the path, bordered by stately plane trees and looking down at crops growing in fields reclaimed from the nearby sea.

Finally we arrive at Beavoir and an open restaurant serving - you guessed it - moules and frites. How can we refuse? The French, perhaps more than any other nation, value food that is grown locally and eaten seasonally. They're a valuable antidote to the marauding globalisation of the food industry. While the rest of the developed world eats food shipped in from the other side of the globe, the wise French continue to treasure food that is grown locally and bears the name of its region. Witness the long-running court battles to protect champagne as a name given to sparkling wine only grown in one particular region. If a vintner in Chile or Australia can call their sparkling drop 'champagne' then all hope is lost for recognising the value of where and how a product is grown and produced.

It's our intention to eat and drink as locally as possible, sampling the delights of each region we ramble through. And today, it's seafood.

The stone walled Restaurant de la Gallette is ideally located on the main road leading to Mont Saint-Michel. It has outdoor tables, but we've spent long enough in the sun and are happy to be ushered inside by a smiling waitress dressed in jeans and a black t-shirt. Today's menu offers two courses - the aforementioned mussels and chips followed by a choice of dessert crepes. For the princely sum of 12.90 euro, Cathie and I are both offered a large blue ceramic bowl of moules in a white wine and leek broth. The crisp golden frites are served on a separate plate. At a nearby table, a young girl who looks to be eight years old, tucks into an equally large serving of mussels. Her less-adventurous parents choose steak. Another reason to love the French. Where else would a child be so food-savvy as to delight in eating mussels? She spoons the rich salty broth over the mussels and slides another one into her mouth.

Our crepe arrives and is filled with apples, in season. They're tart and not too sweet. We wash down this delicious banquet with a bowl of cider. Mussels, leeks, potato and apples - the complete meal in four ingredients, all produced within fifty kilometres of this restaurant.

It's a pleasant few kilometres along the coast to our auberge. We're early but the young man at reception readily books us into a room overlooking corn fields and the bay. We quickly shower and change into more suitable sight-seeing attire and coax Craig and Jenny the extra kilometre along a dirt path to the entry for Mont Saint-Michel. A sign in multiple languages forbids bicycles. Visitors can only enter on foot or in the buses periodically making the two kilometre trek along the newly-erected road to the ancient site. It's a stupid rule, but we do as we're told and begin the long walk along the boardwalk. We're regularly passed by people riding bicycles. I swear under my breath. That's what I deserve for being a conformist.

Mont Saint-Michel is an island six hundred metres off the coast, linked to the mainland by a bridge and levee. It's served a dual role as a military fortification and a monastery since the 8th century. Pilgrims could visit the Abbey at low tide, yet it proved impregnable to invading armies. During the One Hundred Years War, it was successfully defended by only a small garrison.

I've always been a little confused by the One Hundred Years War, which actually continued for one hundred and sixteen years for the pedants out there. Didn't they get tired? Or bored? After each hate-filled generation died out, why didn't they call a truce? Could they remember who started it in the first place?

Nowadays, French footballers regularly invade the English Premier League with a certain Continental panache while the English send thousands of ex-pats across the Channel to renovate old farm houses and settle in ancient villages.

Like many tourist icons, Mont St Michel is surrounded by a tacky enclave of shops and restaurants selling pre-heated food and plastic toys. It's a relief to enter the labyrinth of empty rooms and dark chapels. The spartan interior gives the place a cold stone presence, a proper reflection of the austere life of the monks and pilgrims who lived here centuries ago. We wander through the Knights Hall and the Abbey before stepping out onto the open terrace which offers a stupendous view out to sea. It's here every tourist eagerly waits to see when the tide will turn. Will those people on horseback trotting along the sands make it back to safety before the strongest tides in Europe surge towards land? I look up at the marvellous gold sculpture of the archangel Michael brandishing a sword atop the 32-metre high spire, a suitably Gothic centrepiece in this UNESCO World Heritage Site.

On one stone staircase, I poke my head out of a narrow window and remember that this fortress was also used a prison in ancient times. Where the tides offered protection from invading armies, they were an effective deterrent for any escapees. I shiver at the thought of being stranded in these dark and cold rooms. Still, it's better than being trapped forever in the hellhole that is the lower town. Want to buy another plastic sword? Or perhaps an 'I love Mont Saint-Michel' t-shirt?

Shudder.

We eat dinner in our auberge. It's crowded with a busload of Chinese tourists all herded into a separate dining room. As the paddocks around the Mont are filled with grazing sheep, I choose saltbush lamb. It's delicious. Cathie has a Normandy omelette - a puffy beret-shaped concoction that is both light and oozy. We share a cheese plate for dessert. I once asked a friend in Paris how many cheeses there were in France. He smiled and answered, 'Three hundred and sixty-five. One for every day of the year.' I sneakily walk through the room full of Chinese diners. They are eating sweet desserts of creme brûlée or chocolate mousse. They all look very happy.

Chapter Two:

Lower Normandy, France

Our auberge is more highway motel than quaint French accommodation, but I overlook this inconvenience at breakfast where they offer a vast cornucopia of food, no doubt aware they have to cater for many nationalities and palates. The scrambled eggs are delicious and coffee flows readily from a machine. In every other country I'd prefer my coffee hand-made, but the French are notoriously poor baristas. They do wonders with food, but for some inexplicable reason, their coffee tastes like a cross between fly spray and mud. From a machine, it's acceptable.

We load Craig and Jenny long before the Chinese have woken and set off along the quiet D275. Mont Saint-Michel rises through the mist as we turn off the D road onto a narrow back lane bordered by green fields. In ten kilometres of lazy cycling, we see no cars and yet there's a plethora of Chambre d'Hotes, revelling in the proximity to the ancient monument. They range from cheap and cheerful converted barns to a luxury and regal house set amid sculptured gardens and duck ponds. Through glass windows at the front, I spy well-dressed couples eating breakfast, served by men in crisp white shirts. It's a pastel smorgasbord of elegant clothes and coiffured hair.

Cows and sheep graze on the salt flats, flocks of birds signature across the sky and I can't think of a more pleasant way to spend a morning. We turn south and breeze into Pontaubault, where in 1944 General Patton's troops crossed the old bridge. Victory was still a year away, with the Germans launching numerous counter-attacks on this strategic pont but the line held and soon after Patton lead his troops into Brittany and towards the Loire river.

We stop at a picnic table beside the Selune river to take a photo of the famous old bridge. At precisely the moment I look into the viewfinder, a peloton of cyclists sweeps across the 17th century pont. Their peaked caps flash across the photo. They turn onto our side road and each of the riders chorus 'bonjour' as they race past. A village where cyclists outnumber cars. Perfect.

So begins another section of EU-sponsored voie verte bordered by trees. The houses have flowering window boxes, green lawns scattered with garden beds and children's toys, wood stacks and neat hedges.

The village of Ducey has a lovely 17th century chateau of modest proportions. At the main roundabout, a garden bed of red and white flowers sprouts around an ornamental bicycle. A town worth stopping for coffee. The main street is closed for a market. We walk Craig and Jenny through the crowds among the stalls featuring the dirtiest yet most appetising carrots I've ever seen. I buy a few and put them in the panniers for later.

Fish, meat, cheese, vegetables, shoes, the latest gardening tools - the French one-stop department store is a community gathering of old ladies with shopping trolleys and men sitting in cafes drinking impossibly bad coffee. So we join them at a fetching establishment where an overweight surly man behind the counter creates a diabolical flavour out of Italian Lavazza coffee. I can't complain. It costs less than a euro and my table on the terrace allows me to watch the early morning activity.

A lady in a navy-blue cardigan wheels a white shopping trolley in one hand and holds the lead of her pet dog in the other. Two bent old ladies lean in for the customary three-cheek kiss, their husbands quiet by their sides. A labrador pants wearily beside its owner, both checking out the latest in winter fashion from the stall erected over a Peugeot van. I'm not sure of the average age of the French village, but I'd guess it's much older than the nearby cities. This morning young people are as scarce as good coffee.

Back on the path, Craig begins complaining. His back brake cable fails to release properly and no matter how much I adjust it, he continues to cause problems. He demands a new cable. I consult the map. Saint-Hilaire-du-Harcouet is thirty minutes ride away. I check my watch. Velo shops close for lunch. We pick up the pace and make it to the shop just in time. The friendly young man offers to replace Craig's cable immediately, just before we both think about lunch. I take the opportunity to use the bicycle shop foot pump to inflate all the tyres which have been showing signs of weariness.

It's easy to choose a lunch stop at Saint-Hilaire. The Le Florivan Restaurant is crowded with diners ranging from road workers in overalls to men in business shirts to six women at a long table. We sit under an umbrella and watch the traffic slowly pass. We choose the formula menu - three courses for a very reasonable 11.90 euro.

First course is a hefty slice of ripe rockmelon. It's delicious and again I'm reminded of the French attitude to food. What other country would accept a slice of rockmelon as an entree? But here, it's fresh and in season and everyone eats it down to the rind. Main course is roast pork with mustard sauce accompanied by pasta, the secret is in the wonderful sauce. Baked custard for dessert rounds off this simple tasty meal. All of the tables are occupied at 1pm as this town relaxes in the genuine community of a long lunch. I sip my beer and amuse myself reading the advertisements on the tourist office window. The accordion player, Isabelle Debarre is playing here next Saturday while the town hall hosts an exhibition of photographs of horses. No rock bands or rappers. Accordions and art.

Back on the path, a herd of cows use their tails as lassoes swatting flies as we slowly climb an abandoned train line converted into a bike path. The only sounds are a distant tractor and the buzz of insects as we cycle past old stone barns amid the smell of pine and new mown hay.

We arrive at Romagny in the late afternoon and find our hotel, a simple one-star establishment on the edge of town at a intersection of two D-roads. The owners are a friendly couple, he with cheeky eyes and a jaunty smile while his wife flashes tattoos and earrings. She shows us to our basic room overlooking a garden.

And so begins the daily tedium of washing cycling clothing in the bathroom sink and draping it around the room. Coat hangers are at a premium, so lamps and heaters quickly become decorated with lycra. The joys of a long-distance cyclist.

We eat dinner at the hotel restaurant, sharing a table with an English couple, Ian and Nicole who own a house in a nearby village. They tell us of the joys and pitfalls of living a simple French rural existence. Ian talks about his previous job as an engineer in the sewers of London and his love of bicycles - not for cycling, but for their sheer beauty. I'm gobsmacked to learn he owns five bikes, yet rarely rides them. He knows nothing of the lovely voie verte passing through his home village. For him, the bicycle is a technological marvel. For me, it's a mechanical jigsaw puzzle. Nicole begins a long monologue on why they love France, which can best be summed up in one phrase.

'It's what England used to be like,' she says.

'Respect, manners, small communities, rural living ...' Ian adds.

Ian and Nicole are thoughtful intelligent people searching for a life measured by values rather than money in the bank. I enjoy their company very much. As we eat a delicious creme brûlée, Ian talks about his love of steam-driven tractors. A true English eccentric.

Early the next morning, the hotel owners take our photo as we load Craig and Jenny. They wave as we set out on the slow uphill path along a disused train track. I duck underneath an orchestra of cobwebs spanning the path as we cycle above corn fields and bubbling streams. We climb one hundred and fifty metres in the first ten kilometres. It's a sparkling morning of wispy high clouds and the sun rays filtering through our tree-lined canopy. Pumpkin and corn are bursting to be picked. We follow the old Mortain-Vire railway line which was built in 1887 by the famed engineer Fulgence Bienvenue, father of the Paris underground. Passenger services on this line ceased in 1938 but it was used for freight until 1988 before finally being converted to a cycle path.

After a rollicking downhill, we stop at a beautifully restored railway station converted into a glass-enclosed picnic area, complete with toilets. Very civilised. Many of the railway stations along this route are now private houses. I can only imagine the joy of living on the voie verte, being able to wheel Craig out every morning for a spin along this atmospheric path.

At Vire, we struggle up the steep hill to the centre ville to buy two chocolate eclairs for morning tea and a crusty baguette and camembert which I place in my panniers to slowly melt and ripen for lunch in two hours.

Somehow, in diverting to Vire we lose the velo path and instead find ourselves on a back road among corn fields. The road undulates between sleepy villages. After consulting a map for the third time in ten minutes, I resign myself to following this winding D-road all the way to Campeaux. That's a rather complicated way of saying we are lost, but on a day as bright and cheery as this, I don't mind.

Much of the land in Lower Normandy is devoted to dairy cattle producing cream and butter and of course, the famed Camembert that I carry in my rear pannier. I'm pleased to learn that the average farmer in this region still runs small herds of - on average - thirty cows. The labour of so many farmers goes into producing this remarkable cheese.

Of course, it's not as simple as that. Global corporations are attempting to take over the camembert market and indeed, already control a sizeable share. The French farmer is fighting back by arguing that quality can only be achieved through simple age-old methods that are the antithesis of global corporations. Known as 'the camembert wars' - the battleground is on how the cheese is made, whether produced with raw or pasteurised milk. The industrial giants want pasteurised, the traditionalists argue that camembert has always been, and should always remain, a product of raw milk.

By using pasteurised milk, the giants can't apply the prestigious AOC-label to their cheeses. They want to change the rules. So far, the courts have ruled in favour of the local Grand Cru producers. As I searched for a camembert in the cheese shop in Vire, I made sure I chose one with a *de Lait Cru* label. Give me raw milk and the small farmer over an industrial behemoth any day.

In the tiny village of St Martin Don, under a canopy of trees opposite an elegant little church, we unpack the precious cheese from its round wooden container made from poplar. I break the baguette into sizeable chunks and we eat a delicious cheap French lunch, thinking of all the small farmers who work long hours with the small herds to produce the wonder that is camembert. Long may they reign.

After Campeaux, we follow another back road and quickly realise we are lost yet again. Twice in one day is just clumsy. I'm trying to avoid cycling on the busy D-road, but after looking at the hills we'll face on this sleepy lane, decide to return to the horrors of trucks and vans and speeding Citroens until we arrive at Torigni-sur-Vire where a dark-haired woman in a boulangerie serves me an excellent cafe éclair and fills my water bottle from the tap even though she sells Evian. At Conde-sur-Vire, we finally stumble upon the river cycle path, following it past disused overgrown locks and wild pear trees dangling heavy fruit over the water. Do trout eat poire? Fisherman sit in the shade smoking cigarettes or listening to the radio, waiting. The endless waiting that is the sport of fishing.

The path becomes busy with walkers and joggers which means we're approaching Saint-Lo. The town is the capital of the Manche region of Normandy and was occupied by the Germans in 1940, suffering through terrible bombing raids by the Allies. Samuel Beckett labelled the city *capital of the ruins*. Most of the historic buildings were levelled in the Battle of Normandy. So complete was the devastation, that one American soldier was heard to remark, 'We sure liberated the hell out of this place.'

It's perhaps appropriate that our accommodation for the evening is a sterile highway hotel on the hill just outside of town. The friendly woman at reception pours us a beer and we relax on the rear deck overlooking the car park and an Italian restaurant, the only eating house within walking distance. Guess what we're eating tonight?

French pizzas tend to be too heavy on the cheese but this establishment has a chef with a light touch who makes an excellent calzone. We eat apple sorbet with calvados for dessert and when the waiter forgets to add it to our bill and I remind the owner, he smiles and says 'cadeaux' with a nonchalant flourish. Merci monseiur!

One advantage of staying at a business hotel is the size and variety of the buffet breakfast the next morning. We are most definitely the only people dressed in lycra at this hour. The same woman as yesterday is still working. I imagine her hours are from 6am to 6pm. She seems unnaturally chirpy as she releases Craig and Jenny from their overnight rest in a plush conference room, no less. Unfortunately, Craig does not show appropriate appreciation for this privilege. He has a flat tyre. Merde! I hurriedly pump the tyre, hoping it's not a puncture while businessmen hop into black BMWs and white Audis. We set off back to the river and Craig reckons his tubes have grown fragile after a year housed in a French barn. I answer that Jenny seems to be functioning alright and Craig goes sullen. Such a temperamental bicycle. Some would say he's like his owner.

The morning is very misty and two dairy cows watch us clatter past their wet field. They stare in dignified silence as Craig and I sag along the path. The tyre is slowly deflating. I pump some more and warn him that if this continues, I'll be looking in bicycle stores for a more reliable companion. Craig giggles under his breath. He knows I'd never sell him. We've been through too many European journeys together.

A man in full-length wet-weather gear wades into the middle of the stream and casts a line. The sound of a distant train leaks through the heavy mist. I stop to check Craig's back tyre and Cathie laughs when she catches up.

'What?'

'You have drops of mist on your eyebrows and beard,' she says.

I look at the hair on my legs, glistening with droplets.

'Frosty man!' I say.

At St Fromond, American flags line the bridge and, soon after, a delicious pain de raison and almond croissant line our stomachs. This year marks the 70th anniversary of the D-Day landings and every village is recognising the sacrifice of the American troops.

We're served coffee by a large man with a walrus moustache and curly hair. He looks like a cross between an 80's pop star and a B-grade movie actor. We sit outside the cafe and wait for the mist to lift. I pump some more air into Craig's tyre and promise not to threaten him anymore. He maintains a dignified silence.

In Saint Jean de Daye, Craig's tube finally gives up. I remove his panniers and repair the tube, aided by a sink full of water in the public facilities. I can never locate the puncture unless I immerse the tube in water. Overjoyed to be back in one piece, Craig leads us along a slow canal to Carenton ... where we don't want to be. Lost is becoming the default location of this trip. All because I refuse to carry detailed maps. I want to look at the scenery, not a piece of paper. So we resign ourselves to the extra kilometres my waywardness entails. We eventually find our way to the town of Isigny, ancestral home of Walt Disney. The town has a splendid Hotel de Ville fronting an extensive park where we sit and eat our second consecutive lunch of baguette and camembert.

As we leave town, we're followed by three young Englishmen on bicycles. They're cycling from Cherbourg to Ouistreham and averaging a comfortable forty kilometres a day. It's the final week of holidays before they have to return to University in Newcastle. They seem extremely impressed when I tell them we cycled one hundred kilometres yesterday. But then, they're camping in tents and we're slumming it in hotels, so the extra kilometres is the least we can achieve. They stick to the main road while Cathie and I turn left and follow the D200 back towards the coastline.

At Grandcamp-Maisy, we finally see the English Channel - a lovely vista of calm water, sailing boats and seagulls. Along the D514 two old ladies pick wild berries. Why not? I rest Craig against a post and scramble over the ditch to taste a few juicy samples. I pick a few extra and frantically cycle to offer them to Cathie.

'How do you know they haven't been sprayed,' she says.

'It's France,' I say, 'they treat wild food as ... food, not weeds.'

She takes the berries and eats them.

'And I trust old ladies,' I add, perhaps unnecessarily.

We visit the Pointe Hoc War Memorial on the highest point between Omaha Beach to the west and Utah Beach to the east. This bluff was heavily fortified by the Germans in preparation for any Allied invasion. On D-Day, the US Army scaled the cliffs and captured the position.

Today the battleground is a shrine of rusting metal, piles of concrete and bunkers dark and gloomy. It's left unadorned save for an explanatory sign here and there. What first captures my attention are the numerous bomb craters. There's hardly any flat earth left, just pock-marked ground and crumbling cliffs. Heroically, the US Ranger battalions successfully scaled those cliffs while under heavy German resistance. Tragically, there were high casualties.

Back on the D-road, we stop at the majestic World Peace Statue, a glistening steel sculpture of a winged goddess. The plaque nearby tells the story of Sergeant Frank Peregory, a member of the 3rd Battalion who under heavy fire attacked a German sentry post and successfully captured thirty-five enemy soldiers. How does one man capture so many soldiers? For this extraordinary act, he was awarded the US Medal of Honor.

We ride slowly downhill to Omaha Beach, a long wide sweep of sand. The scene of so much bloodshed seven decades ago is now where children build sandcastles and fly kites, men lounge in beach chairs reading newspapers while ladies in floppy hats walk the dog. Every second house proudly flies an American flag.

We arrive at our hotel which boastfully promotes itself as a *beach resort* and charges accordingly. Three young women work behind the bar in the restaurant. The one with the best English shows us to our cabin, a brightly-painted timber cottage with white tile floors and easy chairs on a covered balcony. The restaurant is closed for lunch, so I make do with a chocolate bar and a beer. Cathie and I stroll along the beach in the afternoon and look back up to the ruins at Pointe Hoc. I remember the barbed wire on top and try to imagine scaling the crumbly cliffs with bullets whizzing past. It's a sacrifice the French have never forgotten.

Out to sea, a lone sailboat tilts on the breeze, its white spinnaker billowing. A flock of gulls hover near the cliffs and a single dog bounds along the sand, chased by a teenage boy in shorts and a t-shirt. He calls twice and the dog stops, trailing a lead from the collar. The boy grabs the lead and smiles at us. Both he and the dog are panting heavily.

Our resort offers dinner and we dutifully comply, because there's very little on offer in Saint Laurent. We both order an appetising chevre chaud salad. I eat lots of complimentary bread because the prices of seafood on the menu are making my eyes water. Salad and bread it is. And beer.

We sleep soundly with the wind whipping off the Channel. Somewhere in the distance a dog barks, a flag poles rattles and the memory of thousands of soldiers live on in the anniversary advertisements, war museums and celebratory signs of a country forever grateful.

We wake at dawn and pack Craig and Jenny in the haze blowing off the water. It's cool and cloudy and the overpriced breakfast is not available for another two hours. All the more reason to start the slow climb up the hill to the promise of a cafe somewhere down the road. Saint Laurent is beautiful this early with only the gulls and wind to accompany us up the hill. The only car we pass on the D514 is a boulangerie delivery van stopped outside a chambre d'hote, selling a basket of croissants to the owner. I wonder if he'd sell us two? We resist and soon enough are passed by the same van. So begins a curious game of hopscotch with the delivery driver. We pass him on three more occasions as he makes his early morning drops. Each time I'm tempted but Cathie believes there'll be a cafe somewhere ahead offering croissants AND coffee.

We ride alongside corn fields and past the 1944 Museum with an American tank near the front entrance. No signs of a cafe. After an hour we risk a long downhill to Port-en-Bessin, a lovely fishing village with a narrow safe harbour full of moored vessels and a ribbon of cafes along the quay. We choose Cafe du Port because of the simple name and the jovial waitress in a blue smock. She offers a very cheap and hugely satisfying petit dejeuner with excellent coffee. Who says the French can't make coffee?

Three men walk into the cafe. All wear fisherman overalls, smoke cigarettes and look very bleary-eyed. One carries a huge live lobster. They sit at the table next to us and order coffee and beer. Is this the authentic fisherman breakfast? Lobster man puts his catch on the floor. Its claws are bound. I imagine they've had a successful night and this prize is for the home pot. The waitress brings her own coffee to their table and joins them, admiring their catch amid much laughter. We contemplate a second coffee and the slow climb to Bayeaux.

Fuelled by an excellent breakfast, we arrive at the Bayeaux Museum just as it's opening and before the busloads of tourists. The Bayeaux Tapestry is justly famous - a one thousand year old embroidered cloth tapestry measuring a mind-boggling seventy metres long depicting the events leading up to the Norman Conquest of England in 1066.

It's displayed behind a glass case for all of its length and reminds me of an ancient movie storyboard, with the bloodthirsty heroic narrative as captivating as any Hollywood epic. So, let me tell the story as a screenwriter would pitch it to a producer.

Edward the Confessor enlists Harold to go to Normandy to tell William he will soon be appointed King. William makes Harry swear an oath of allegiance. Harry returns to find Ed is dead and regally crowns himself as King while nervously looking across the Channel, sure he can already hear the approaching horses of William's vengeful army. So begins the Battle of Hastings - cue heroic sword fights, mud, blood and the odd severed limb. Actually, it was worse than that. The defeated were decapitated and then stripped naked because ... well, in the Middle Ages being dead on a muddy battlefield wasn't enough. You deserved ritual humiliation as well. Even the horses lost their heads. Harry the cheat gets an arrow through the eye for lying to William thereby enshrining the need to always tell the truth, especially to a spiteful warrior who wants to be King. William and his cleric brother Odo, who carries a mace because priests aren't allowed to spill blood but can batter their enemies senseless, are victorious. Bill the Bastard becomes William the Conquerer, proving that being a good soldier can certainly earn you a cool nickname and a starring role in a 1000-year-old wall hanging and the chance that Brad Pitt will play you in the latest Hollywood epic.

We spend an hour following the cloth in its semi-circular tale of bloodshed and heroism. I loved it so much I bought a souvenir of a scene where the horsemen prepare for battle. It seemed appropriate to buy a sunglass case with this motif - Harold getting one through the eye.

We celebrate William's conquering by raiding a nearby boulangerie and eating two excellent almond croissants. We offer the baker a few gold coins for her tasty bounty. She seems content with the transaction.

'Are you going to talk in that fake medieval accent all day,' Cathie says.

'Who says it's fake,' I respond.

'Putting *Ye* in front of every third word doesn't make sense,'

'Oh ye of little faith!'

We ride back to the D514, one of us quiet while the other pretends to be a warrior aboard a proud and gallant steed. Craig creaks in unison with my cries of 'tally ho!' Cathie suggests an appropriate name for her warrior husband would be *Steven the Imbecile*.

Without fanfare, we arrive in Arromanches-les-Bains, the site of the Allies first artificial port which allowed the unloading of heavy artillery on D-day. Sections of the mulberry harbour can still be seen - large concrete blocks now covered with green silt and seaweed. From a distance, in the haze they look like so many beached whales.

Arromanches was also the site in 2013 of a truly remarkable *sand installation* where nine thousand human forms were carved into the beach at low tide, simply by using cut-out stencils and rakes. The sand sculpture commemorated the lives of the nine thousand people who died during the D-day landings. These moving yet simple images were a poignant reminder that as many French civilians were killed as Allied soldiers during the horrors of the first twenty-four hours. The beautiful sculpture was designed to be washed away by the incoming tide, as finally and irrevocably as the loss of human life in war.

And so on to Courseulles-sur-Mer, a fishing village dissected by the river Seulles. It's lunch time and we park Craig and Jenny on the marina where they can admire the bobbing yachts and sailboats. It's easy to choose a restaurant - the Creperie du Port is crowded with diners and has the cheapest menu on this strip. For the princely sum of eight euro, I enjoy a delicious bovine galette with mince, cheese and egg. I'm impressed when the waitress asks me how I'd like my mince cooked. Even the humble beef patty deserves the close attention of the chef. The joy of food is not based on the price but the culture. For dessert, we're swayed by the crepe flambé - a mini-urn of burning calvados poured over a crepe pomme. How can we resist? The dessert arrives at our table with four huge dollops of cream accompanying the pyrotechnics. It tastes as good as it looks. Luxury for a few euros.

Après lunch we cycle along the promenade at Saint-Aubin-sur-Mer. It's a ride back through time with the worn majesty of row after row of stone beach-front houses. The paint is faded, the shutters closed. A woman in an ice-cream van dozes, the radio plays classical music, old men ride rusty bikes with a wobble in the back wheel, fishermen at low tide use a curious square board and net to catch shrimp, old ladies dig in flower gardens and I wonder how much one of these derelict mansions costs. On and on we ride through the receding dreams of a thousand ice-cream vendors and sideshow salesmen until woken from our revelry by the noise and bustle of the ferry terminal at Ouistreham.

Our hotel is directly opposite the lock gates. I fling open the windows to our room and am greeted by the sight of a score of semitrailers lining up to board the cross-Channel ferry. Below our window are two outdoor restaurants - in the late afternoon, people sit under umbrellas drinking beer and watching the Winnebagos fight for space in the parking lot.

To escape the noise, Cathie and I walk up the hill to the church. We sit on wicker chairs near the entrance. A woman dressed in black with a mauve scarf around her shoulders comes in, crosses herself and sits a few rows in front of us. She takes out her mobile phone and makes a call, her loud voice ringing through the empty church. After she hangs up, she walks into the confession booth where she checks her email. Another woman, wearing jeans and a cut-off singlet, enters with a young child dressed in pink. They walk to the statue of the Virgin Mary and the girl lights a candle and offers it to her mother. The woman steps forward and places it at the feet of the statue. She says a quick prayer before they leave. The girl skips out the door. The mobile phone woman, having finished her business also leaves.

We follow her into the fading light. As we walk through the park we notice a policeman at the intersection stopping the occasional car. We can't work out whether he's on duty or just stopping people he recognises to have a quick chat. He doesn't issue any infringement notices. In his smart uniform and beret, he looks every inch the symbol of French bureaucracy. He appears to be enjoying his late afternoon escapade. When a young woman walks by in a short skirt with high heels, the policeman looks furtively in her direction, ignoring the man in the Citroen he was just talking with. A roost of pigeons on the church roof look down disapprovingly.

It's time for dinner.

At a restaurant called La Marine, Cathie enjoys the briny taste of oysters, large and succulent. I make do with coq au vin, accompanied by the ever-present stack of chips. The restaurant is full of English tourists, all waiting for the evening ferry to Portsmouth. Most of them are pensioners. Grey hair, flat-soled shoes and sensible cardigans. They all order dessert.

Saturday morning dawns misty and cool and we return to La Marine for a simple breakfast. There's no sign of the English tourists of the previous evening, just the same waiter ferrying cups of coffee to the locals smoking cigarettes on the footpath.

We cycle along the Caen canal on a lovely path, watching the ducks glide peacefully along the still water. Pegasus Bridge is a strategically important pont where the RAF won a decisive battle in World War Two. A bus pulls up nearby and unloads a gaggle of tourists to view the famous bridge. I expect to hear English accents, but they're all French.

As the mist lifts, a group of men in orange vests line up along a corn field. Each man stands about fifty metres away from his comrade. They all appear to be carrying a wooden club. I'm so intrigued, I turn off the path and ride towards them. Some of the men are also carrying guns. The road is closed. A bright orange sign depicts a running boar. Suddenly a horn blasts and the men slowly and deliberately enter the corn field. I hope they eat the boar if they catch him.

Back on the road, we're passed by a man riding a bright red contraption that looks like a spaceship on bicycle wheels. He cruises past us silently.

Admiring old bridges, hunting wild boar, cycling spaceships - what people do on the weekend.

And so begins our day among the Belle Époque sea front villages of Lower Normandy. At the end of the 19th century, the train from Paris took a comfortable four hours to bring the rich and privileged here to breathe the fresh air.

Cabourg, Dives-sur-Mer and Houlgate are elegant museum pieces. They still attract tourists who walk slowly along the wide promenade and try their luck at waterfront casinos. At Houlgate, the bayside car park is crowded with Winnebagos, their owners walking along the train tracks into the narrow streets of the village crammed with ice-cream shops, cafes and boulangeries. Like everyone, we indulge in a cake and coffee for morning tea. The prices are noticeably higher. The Belle Époque has faded, now the great unwashed make do with a cafe eclair and a flutter at the gaming house. The back streets are crowded with Porsches and Mercedes looking in vain for a parking space. We happily cycle past them and through the last roundabout, decorated with a vivid flower display and one lone blackface statue of a jazz musician welcoming visitors to the Spring Jazz Festival. I'm not sure about the politics of a blackface greeting, but the town is undergoing a revival. Perhaps the lure of the seaside never fades for jaded city dwellers?

We climb a long slow hill before cruising back down to the beach at Villers-sur-Mer where two large topiary dinosaurs stare balefully along the promenade. Is this the easiest ten kilometres of the trip? The promenade is bordered by a wide sandy beach and flowering gardens. We hardly have to pedal, just sit back and watch the passing parade of holidaymakers licking ice-creams, drinking coffee and wearing silly hats.

We make our way to Deauville where the American Film Festival is taking place in large white marquees on the foreshore. Suddenly, the silly hats are replaced by elegant casual wear - flowing linen dresses and Armani suits. Maserati trumps BMW and the promenade is crowded with fake suntans and high heels. Two men in suits with sunglasses and earpieces stand at the entrance to the Festival. Perhaps on guard for bad-tempered film critics? Craig and Jenny and their owners look woefully out of place among the visitors waiting outside. We don't even want to enter, we've just been sucked into the mass of people. I look at an advertising poster for the Festival - I've never heard of any of the American guests. George Clooney visited in 2008. Oh well.

We eventually find our way into the centre ville and are overwhelmed by the rich and would-be rich sunning their fake tans at every outdoor cafe. The only place that is relatively quiet is a small cafe serving bagels. Isn't that American enough for the film buffs? We take a table near the window. The owners are a young couple and it's readily apparent they've just started the business. They eagerly serve each customer, yet haven't quite worked out how the kitchen should function at peak capacity. Our food arrives eventually and it's tasty and good value for this nouveau rich town.

We leave Deauville to its red carpet and best film awards. The exit from town is nowhere near as pleasant as the entry - along a busy D-road beside the train tracks to Paris. We eventually find a quieter route and settle for an afternoon of cycling through farmland among timber vertical-frame dwellings that remind me of gingerbread houses. Wattle and daub construction is so appealing, I keep stopping and taking photos. The ancient building method is undergoing a revival and long may it continue.

At Pont l'Évêque, we order two beers at a sunny outdoor café and wonder how long we have to wait before our accommodation opens. I'd like to nod off for an hour in this sleepy afternoon, but I don't think the waitress would approve of a middle-aged man snoring while his embarrassed wife sips on her Kronenbourg.

Our accommodation is three kilometres out of town. The efficient and friendly owner shows us to our cabin near a barbecue area. The interior is generous and we have a verandah to drape our washing on. The owner laughs heartily when we explain our intention.

In the evening, we cycle into town and spend a long time trying to decide where we'll eat, finally choosing Le Rollon restaurant. It opens at 7.30. It's 7.15 when we peek through the window. The owners, a handsome couple are sitting at a table drinking a glass of wine and sharing a plate of food. At precisely 7.30 they welcome us into their warm interior. By eight o'clock, the room is full. We order the three-course menu for 19:80 euro and are astonished at the elegant simplicity of the food. First course is a Pont l'Évêque cheese fried in a crisp pastry drizzled with local honey and served with a salad of lettuce, tomatoes and walnuts. Pont l'Évêque cheese is an uncooked unpressed cow's milk variety with a white rind. It's been produced in this area for a staggering nine hundred years. And in the hands of a chef as competent as the gentleman in the kitchen, it's delicious.

The husband is the chef, the wife runs the front of house. I watch her all evening. She greets most diners with a kiss. Despite the demands of serving thirty hungry customers, she does everything with a practised efficiency. The ritual of French dining is like watching a scripted piece of casual theatre. Dinner is conversation and food, enjoyed in an unhurried way. The dishes are rich and satisfying but never too large. The French take their time over a meal, savouring every bite. In this way, they know when they've eaten enough. It's so different than the modern trend of upsizing where a meal is measured by quantity not quality.

I will leave this restaurant satisfied and yet not weighed down by unnecessary calories.

Our main course is chicken with a mushroom sauce and a side of potato and cheese gratin. I ask for more bread to sponge up every last drop of sauce. For dessert, we savour a magnificent tarte tartin, an absolute delight of apple and toffee.

When it looks as though the throng of people and dishes will overwhelm our host, her daughter magically appears from upstairs. She is stunningly beautiful and, like her Mum, greets many of the diners with a kiss.

Despite having been here for three hours, we are the first to leave. The waitress shows us to the door and wishes us a good evening. We hop on Craig and Jenny and ride through the quiet streets admiring the full moon rising over the horse paddocks.

Chapter Three:

Upper Normandy - Pont l'Évêque to Ault, France

No matter what time you wake on Sunday morning, it's too early. Pont l'Évêque sleeps as we cycle through the village, casting a wistful eye at La Rollon Restaurant, wishing they served breakfast. Today is Father's Day and I remind Craig that he should play nicely and treat me with due care, for I am twelve thousand miles away from my adult sons who I miss dearly. He appears to understand. We alternate between an abandoned railway-cum-cycle-path and the D675 before rambling along a narrow country lane which we suspect will lead us to Honfleur. It doesn't.

Craig reacts by getting a puncture. So much for Father's Day kindness. After repairing the tube and giving Craig a severe tongue-lashing, my phone beeps with messages from both my sons. I sigh and Cathie promises me a large breakfast in Honfleur. We cruise downhill to the lovely seaside village. Despite the early morning, it's already crowded with tourists walking around the harbour made famous by the Impressionists, Claude Monet and Gustave Courbet.

It's a beautiful amphitheatre of narrow six-storey stone buildings reflected in the calm water of the marina. Sure enough, at one end of the quay, a group of artists have set up easels and are hard at work creating their version of *Honfleur Morning*. These modern amateurs are soul brothers to fly-fishermen - any excuse to spend hours in such a magnificent location. The painters strive to catch the sunlight while I try to catch the eye of the waiter for breakfast. This being a tourist town, the offerings are small, expensive and pedestrian.

Japanese tourists take photos of the artists recreating the scene on canvas. But the true artistry can be found in the elegant lines of the French carousel near the harbour entrance - carved hand-painted horses galloping around a polished wooden platform. While carousels are dismantled and replaced by soulless plastic and aluminium playgrounds elsewhere, the French remain committed to maintaining these historic and joyful marvels. The Honfleur version is a double-deck masterpiece with pure white prancing horses and tiny carriages for would-be princes and princesses.

We mount our own galloping steeds and prance along the feeder road, casting a rather concerned eye at the Pont de Normandie rising over the Seine river. One of the longest cable-stay bridges in the world, it looks devilishly steep and packed with trucks. Up we go. I've never experienced vertigo on a bicycle before. I stop at the highest point and watch the cargo ships heading towards the ocean. A seagull lands on the pylon a few metres away. We look at each other for a few seconds as if to say, 'It's a long way down, Buddy.' I can see the city of Le Havre in the hazy distance. It's only a few kilometres via the motorway, but we're funnelled into a back route via the container terminals. Fifteen lonesome kilometres on a wide and windy road that leads between a bewildering number of oil terminals. I'm pleased it's Sunday and we have the path to ourselves, save for an occasional scurrying rat. It's not the most attractive entry into the second largest port in France. So much water, so many bridges and yet we still can't find the centre ville. Eventually, we end up at the old docks, now renovated into a glass-enclosed mall of outlet shops. I shake my head in wonder. From a noble history as the transport hub of France, loading and unloading everything from wood to wine and coal to tobacco - now just another shopping centre selling tight jeans and American baseball caps.

It's a glorious day and most of the population are at the beach soaking up the last rays of summer. We trace a long line around the foreshore, picking our way past cafes and ice-cream vendors before climbing a steep hill at Sainte-Adresse where an outdoor cafe with umbrellas and a startling view back across the harbour proves too tempting to resist.

As I sit at a table, a waitress approaches and says it's only for diners. I don't understand. She means we must order a meal, not just sit on one cup of coffee while admiring the view. We assure her we'll be eating. She smiles and seeing our cycling attire, immediately brings us two carafes of cold water. Lovely. I order a club sandwich and 'home potatoes.' Cathie has a salad. Both meals are unexpectedly large and tasty and we're tempted to spend the afternoon watching the bikini parade of thin French women strolling to the beach. The men, by comparison, are short and somewhat dumpy. And everyone is smoking.

'Weight loss,' Cathie explains, succinctly.

'They should take up cycling,' I suggest.

We glance at a beautiful blonde woman walking past wearing a wispy blouse and high heels.

'In those shoes,' Cathie smiles.

My iPad map suggests we climb this enormous hill at the rear of the cafe and cycle towards the airport. Damn. It's too hot for hill-climbs. I take off my helmet and clip it around my handlebars. At the speed we'll be travelling, I won't be needing *un casque de velo*. I soak my bandanna with water in the vain hope it'll keep me cool. It isn't so bad. I've had worse experiences. At the dentist, for example. Cathie mentions childbirth, in between gulps of water and cursing.

The land opens up on top of the hill to a tarmac runway and expansive wind-swept fields of corn. A swirling bunch of sky-divers parachute to earth, like slow-dancing tops. From this distance, it appears elegant and serene. If I was clinging to a cord and a lifeline of flimsy nylon two hundred metres above the earth I may think differently. My screams would be heard all over France.

Soon we're thrust onto the D940, the major road along the coast. There's nothing to do but grit our teeth and pedal as fast as we can, hoping for a bike lane sooner or later. It turns out to be later. Much later. The town of Etretat, in fact.

Etretat is justly famous for its chalky limestone cliffs and the three natural arches that have been immortalised in oil on canvas by the Impressionists, Monet, Boudin and Courbet. Two of the three arches can be seen from town, which means the main promenade is crowded with camera-toting tourists all looking for the perfect angle. A phalanx of stand-up boarders (plankers? plonkers?) paddle towards the western arch as if worshipping the jagged geometry. Ice-creams are being devoured in world-record numbers and day walkers clamber to the top of either hill book-ending the beach to witness the splendour that is Etretat on holiday.

It's at these moments I think of God and religion. Do the villagers lucky enough to be born in such a splendid location devoutly attend Mass each Sunday to thank the Lord for their bounty? Which of course begs the question - do the citizens of Yport, the next village along the coast and not blessed with such natural wonder, damn the Lord for giving all the prizes to their neighbours? Or do these forsaken ones attend church even more frequently to pray for erosion to create another archway closer to them? Or pray for mighty storms to batter the coastline and finally crumble the limestone arches at Etretat?

Further to my musings on the mysterious ways of the big fellow upstairs, Etretat is where the young 19th century French novelist Guy de Maupassant helped save the English poet Algernon Swinburne from drowning. Being a typical writer, he penned a short story about the incident.

Sixty years later, the renowned First World War heroes Charles Nungesser and Francois Coli set off from Etretat on a clear Spring morning attempting to fly non-stop from Paris to New York. They were never to be seen again.

Which would lead the cruel and heartless to suggest that God loves poets but doesn't much care for daredevil aviators. Perhaps it's because they soar too close to his domain?

Such deep and meaningful thoughts always lead me to one destination - the boulangerie. This afternoon I worship a beatific café eclair, crossing myself twice before devouring every tasty morsel. Cathie makes do with a can of coke. Her eyes look towards the next D-road. It's uphill all the way.

'The Lord giveth ...' I begin.

Her look stops today's sermon immediately.

The climb out of Etretat is marvellous, along a quiet winding road that overlooks a narrow green valley where ... oh my ... a steam train slowly ascends. The engine man obliges by tooting his whistle. I turn to Cathie. She's smiling. She knows how much I like trains of any description. I wistfully attempt to keep pace with my friend the tiny locomotive as we both chug into Les Loges. Time for a photo of the oversized child in lycra standing in front of a steam train. I remember it's Father's Day and silently shed a tear. A steam train whistle doesn't replace hugs from two sons, but I'll take whatever comfort I can.

So begins a magical late afternoon cycling along a high plateau through rolled-haybale fields where three generations of families are out walking the narrow lanes. A sleepy Sunday haze descends over the countryside. I take one hand off the handlebars and start singing. Cathie drops further behind but I suspect it's not due to fatigue.

After one hundred and five kilometres and seven hours in the saddle, we arrive at our auberge for the evening. The sparse yet comfortable room is above a barn where the owner thoughtfully wheels Craig and Jenny. I forgot to ask her not to place Craig near spiderwebs. He's a little scared of *une araignee*. I'm sure Jenny will protect him.

We had hoped the auberge provided dinner, but as it's Sunday the owner has unilaterally given herself a well-earned respite. So we ask her to phone the local pizza restaurant for home delivery. A bottle of rose and pizza. Who says there isn't a God!

Cecile, the owner is a young woman with a husband, two children and a barn full of old cars and bicycles. In the early morning, Craig has forgiven me my sins for swearing at him yesterday and pushing him well past his usual comfort zone. What on earth was I thinking? He slept the night in a spider-free barn accompanied by Jenny and the owner's six - count them - six bicycles! Craig no doubt regaled them with exaggerated stories of his exploits throughout Europe, even going so far as to boast about having climbed one of the highest Italian Alps. I get the impression the silent six are relieved when I wheel him away. Jenny rolls her tyres and seems to say, 'it's how he is ...' She's heard all his stories before.

We leave them in the meek sunlight while Cecile offers us a delicious breakfast of home-made yoghurt, cheeses, prunes, figs and the usual baked suspects.

'The perfect accompaniment to a full breakfast is a long hill climb,' I say as we begin our ascent of *Col de Fecamp*. It isn't really a French mountain pass, but this early in the morning it certainly feels like one. Fecamp, according to legend, is where a tree trunk carrying the blood of Christ was washed ashore in the 1st century.

I love these stories.

Cathie and I once attended a church in Bruges, Belgium where a vial containing a cloth stained with Christ's blood is venerated. We sat among the congregation as the Priest held the vial aloft. There were only twenty worshippers. It struck me that if this really was Christ's blood, the church would be packed to the rafters with people praying for miracles and forgiveness and redemption and blessing and for FC Bruges to finally win a Belgium football championship.

Fecamp is a working harbour, undecided as to whether its most profitable catch is fish or tourists. The morning sun struggles against an onshore breeze and an intemperate haze. We navigate another hill and Craig asks for the third time how many kilometres I'm proposing for today. I tell him an easy sixty.

'Easy for who,' he mutters.

'Easy for whom,' I respond. I can't abide a bicycle with poor speech.

The fields smell of leek, ready for harvesting. Piles of compost steam from a communal village heap. An unwritten rule in France is that the smaller the village, the longer the name. I offer three nearby exhibits.

Ancretteville-sur-Mer.

Sassetot-le-Mauconduit.

Saint-Martin-aux-Bunveaux.

These villages have fewer residents than letters in their names.

We round a corner and see a row of people taking a photo of something just out of view. Chateau de Sissy is a three-storey pink and white pile set back from the road with a splendid front garden of grass and roses. I count sixteen tiny windows on the top floor. For servants or extended families?

'You could build a football field in that garden,' I say.

Cathie pushes Jenny into the frame of my photo and attempts a smile.

'If it's not food, it's football with you,' she says.

'The magical *f*?' I say.

We later learn that the 18th century chateau on eleven hectares is a hotel. It looks romantic and alluring from the outside, but numerous reviews complain of small dark rooms and aloof service. Which proves you can't judge a chateau by its facade. I took photos of Cathie and Jenny at the front gates as if they were about to regally breeze along the driveway and demand the Presidential Suite.

We cruise down a steep hill through a glade of horse paddocks. The *Cyclist-Principle* is that each downhill is followed by an uphill. So far this morning we're averaging a snail-pace 13 kph. A portly man on a clapped-out Peugeot could do better than that? At Paluel, we ignore the nuclear reactor towering above us and climb yet another hill in the wind. At Aeroport Saint-Valery, the only building is a bar near the runway. Now I'm not one to criticise, but should an aeronautical club be encouraging drinking before take-off? The single plane near the tarmac looks rather old and small - perhaps the only person in danger is the pilot of the single-seater?

It's downhill all the way to Saint-Valery and the chance of lunch. Any restaurant called 'l'Eden' wins my vote and we're fortunate to get the last available table indoors. At the next table, an old lady with too much make-up wears a flowing white dress and her hair is gathered flamboyantly atop her head. Her husband has white hair and wears a natty beige suit. They greet us warmly despite our lycra lowering the tone of the restaurant considerably. Madam eats oysters before moving onto a large bowl of mussels. Her husband begins with salmon before selecting a large piece of whitefish for the main course. We stick to the formula menu - pate followed by rabbit in white sauce. And coffee burnt beyond recognition. I gulp it down. Perhaps I'm developing an immunity?

The host brings us the bill and in French asks where we're from. I answer, 'Je suis Australian.' He asks if we speak English and I'm tempted to answer, 'better than the English.' We bid farewell to the elderly couple who are studying the dessert menu.

The waterfront is utterly deserted. Even the Casino is empty. We climb yet another hill, this one framed by majestic trees. It's so beautiful, as Cathie rode away I stopped and snapped a photo of the scene. It nows graces the front cover of this book.

Our accommodation this evening is the Chalet La-Chapelle-sur-Dun, a rambling three-storey homestead with high ceilings and elegant faded furniture that only the French could get away with. Except our host is American. Jeff shows us upstairs to our corner room. It's almost as large as our house back in Australia. We glory in the afternoon sun coming through the tall windows and contemplate whether to fall asleep or drink numerous aperitifs before our evening meal. Or both?

Craig and Jenny rest in the garden under a tree near the tennis court. I can hear Craig whining from here. He knows we plan to leave them outdoors overnight and he is not pleased. When I finish my next drink, I will attend my steed. After one glass too many, Cathie and I amuse ourselves by taking photos posing next to the numerous paintings hanging in our room. The artist is Jeff's mother, now sadly deceased. She knew her way around an easel with a particular fascination for vases of flowers and summer beach scenes.

For dinner, we buy a baguette, a tin of tuna, two tomatoes, a lettuce and a bottle of white wine and eat at a rickety table in the garden as the birds serenade and the hearty thwack of a racquet on a tennis ball rents the evening gloom. Craig can be heard warning Jenny of a descending mist and biting insects. Does he ever stop?

We sleep in a bed bigger than many Tahitian islands.

The croissants for breakfast are so light I think they may well float away, so I eat them quickly. Jeff offers us another cup of coffee and as he's not French, we happily agree. When an American can beat a French person in the kitchen, you know something is wrong.

Craig is less angry than I thought he'd be. In fact, he liked camping under a tree in the garden with a full moon. The household cats kept away and he and Jenny enjoyed a romantic interlude. He's positively spritely this morning, even suggesting that perhaps Cathie and I should 'camp out' rather than indulging in a soft bed with cotton sheets each night. I tell him we'll think about it.

On a blue sky morning we ride through sugar beet fields down to the tourist resort of Pourville-sur-Mer which houses an oyster farm near the promenade. They grow them, sell them and eat them all in the one building. L'Huitriere has pride of place on the foreshore. Diners can slurp oysters and study the distant cliffs. And perhaps spy two puffing cyclists climbing yet another hill. Look there now, one of them is waving. Do they always wave with one finger in Australia?

We enter the hill-top suburbs outside Dieppe where workers are adding a new awning to a double-storey mansion. The gardener clips a hedge and encourages Cathie as she climbs yet another incline. I take a quick photo of the thatched roof house he calls home. I wonder what sound the rain makes on a thatched roof? And does the owner live in perpetual fear of a fire? Perhaps I'm showing my background, for we come from the most fire-prone continent on earth. The indigenous culture used fire as a way of regenerating the land. They didn't build wooden houses among the trees like we later arrivals have done.

In green and rural France, we are a long way from the wildfires of native Australia. I applaud the gardener his rustic and beautiful choice of roofing material.

Our first stop in Dieppe is for cake and coffee at a cafe made famous by Oscar Wilde. When not writing bon mots and timeless plays, the Englishman hung out at the Cafe des Tribunaux, in exile after the scandals back in old Blighty. It's here he began his last great work, The Ballad of Reading Gaol. It's a suitably flamboyant venue for dear Oscar with lots of stained glass, wrought iron and a bronze statue of Lady Justice taking pride of place in the centre of the room. Ironic really, given the reception that was afforded the English customer when his true identity was finally revealed. But more on that shortly.

Today, Dieppe is hosting a kite festival on the beach. We cycle along the promenade underneath billowing nylon creatures - a red and black striped fish, a rainbow-coloured bird, a blue and white shark and perhaps my favourite, a three-metre long floating banana. Children and cyclists stare and point and clap their hands in glee. It's funny how a simple thing can colour one's perception of a town. From drab to colourful in twenty pieces of fluttering fabric.

Oscar Wilde retreated to nearby Berneval-le-Grand following his unmasking in Dieppe. He threw an ill-judged party inviting the local boy's schoolmaster and his charges, but not the corresponding girls school. The party went well. The aftermath did not. The citizens of

Berneval were not thrilled to discover they had a *savage* on their doorstep, no matter how many foreigners claimed he was a genius. Oscar soon departed for Paris where he died, bankrupt and alone a few years later.

There is little sign of genius in today's lunch, but with three courses for twelve euro there certainly is quantity. Keno flashes in the corner and everyone drinks beer, including the muscular row of truck drivers at the bar. I'm a little nervous about getting back on Craig and facing the rigours of the D113. But before that, the waitress offers us dessert. As dear Oscar would say, 'I can resist anything but temptation.'

To dodge the wandering truck drivers, we choose a potato field back road all the way to Le Treport, justly famous for *fruits de mer* and towering chalky-white cliffs. Even more blinding than the limestone cliffs is the display of white linen casual-wear at one clothes shop. Do people actually wear clothes that white? We escape the bling fest to Mers les Bains, the slightly more genteel neighbour across the bay. While Le Treport boasts industry and seafood, Mers les Bains claims Jules Verne, Victor Hugo and Gustave Eiffel as visitors in the distant past. It has an alluring row of four-storey timber mansions on the esplanade and impossibly cute white-painted change-huts scattered along the rocky beach. It's all very summertime 1974. I even see someone wearing a kaftan. They're about to get into a Karman Ghia.

We could use the iconic sports car to get us up the next hill, but make do with lots of huffing and puffing and the firm promise to my beautiful wife that tomorrow we will cycle less kilometres and it'll be all downhill.

We arrive at tonight's accommodation to be greeted by a locked gate and two snarling German Shepherds. I push every button on the entry pad but no-one comes to meet us. We look at the dogs. The canines bark at us. Detente.

Eventually, the owner arrives in a silver Mercedes clutching a whip and a large chair. Using a remote control, she opens the gate and beats the snarling savages back with the whip. True. I still have the marks to prove it. The supine dogs lick her outstretched hand and pretend to be cuddly.

Convinced we aren't lycra-clad intruders, Madam shows us our room for the evening and offers to dial-a-pizza for our dinner. Yet again I have booked a room miles from any restaurant. The owner has second thoughts about our suitability as house guests when I cover our front balcony with dripping clothes. Sans clothes line, it's the balcony or the lampshade. Fearing fire, I choose the balcony and the last rays of evening light.

We eat the pizza - too much cheese not enough salami - on the very same balcony and wonder why all the other guests stay indoors. Such a lovely evening. Such beautiful underwear.

Chapter Four

Upper Normandy - Ault to Berck-sur-Mer, France

We're beginning to be lulled into a false sense of European weather. For the tenth straight day, we wake to clear skies and the forecast of mild temperatures. We celebrate our good fortune with an extra croissant and two slices of baguette smothered in home-made strawberry confiture. Madam walks us to the gate. One of her German Shepherds dribbles on my ankle, to remind me of yesterday's misunderstanding.

This morning, we break all previous records by getting lost within the first five hundred metres. We cruise down a very steep hill to the water at Bois de Cise expecting to discover a beach road leading us to Ault.

No.

Back up the hill and along the D940 sees us bucketing down the correct road into Ault. On the distant water's edge at low tide, scores of locals with buckets are fossicking for seafood gold. Four ladies, dressed in wellington boots, jeans and jackets come up from the beach carrying their bounty. They're only too pleased to show us their catch. Each woman displays half-a-bucket full of mussels. I ask if I can take a photo. They line up proudly along the seawall, with the blonde woman at the end tilting her bucket so her mussels can be seen. Not to be outdone, she offers to take our photo. I mockingly grab a bucket. A fisherman in lycra.

All this is done while the town eccentric, a middle-aged man wearing knee-high socks, an ill-fitting cardigan and a Greek fisherman's cap jabbers away in the background. At first, I try to include him in the stilted French-English conversation, but quickly realise he's talking more nonsense than the rest of us combined. He seems quite happy to mutter away to himself. I think he even poked his head into one of our photos.

The women go off to contemplate mussels and frites for lunch while Cathie and I slowly pedal away from the gentleman with the endearing disposition. Ault is a lovely town set above the ocean. Many of the stone houses have been painted a jaunty colour and given a particular name. We pass *Freya, Marianne* and *l'Oasis* on the way out of town.

The cliffs give way to swamp land near Cayeux-sur-Mer which boasts a rock factory at either end of the town. Piles of ocean-smoothed rocks wait to be hauled away to decorate gardens. They do little to enhance the appeal of this desolate seaside village. We can't even find a boulangerie.

We join the busy D3 for a rushed pedal into Saint-Valery-sur-Somme, a beguiling village of ancient ramparts, Gothic church, handsome town square and perhaps the best almond croissants known to humankind. We scoff them ravenously and consider ordering a half-dozen for this afternoon. Before we can, there's a frantic commotion down on the boardwalk. Crowds gather, cameras are readied and people push for the best position.

The tide rushes into the estuary. A lone kayaker rides the cascade all the way past scores of people on the boardwalk cheering his every stroke. He hardly needs to paddle, so strong is the current. The Bay of the Somme has the largest tidal range in the region, boasting changes of up to ten metres during a full moon. We've been privileged to witness a tidal change while scoffing our second, or is that third, almond croissant.

Next in line to audition for *the many charms of Saint-Valery* is a steam train pulling into the station. The locomotive and three carriages run around the bay from Saint-Valery to Le Crotoy. A lycra-clad cyclist eagerly takes photos of overweight tourists hanging out of each red and cream-painted carriage. Everyone on board is smiling. Saved from the iron knackery by an association of train enthusiasts, the *Chemin der Fer de la Baie de Somme* now fulfils the dreams of 90,000 tourists each year.

So invigorated by the charms of Saint-Valery, we power along the bicycle path towards Le Crotoy ... and Craig gets a puncture. He could see I was having too much fun and wanted to remind me of the travails of cycling.

Correction, *the travails of Craig.*

I repair the puncture and set off at a slightly reduced pace. A handsome young man sits next to a row of hire bicycles. Using elaborate mime, I ask if I can borrow his foot pump. He willingly helps me pump up Craig's errant tube. Having spied his vast array of tools, I suggest he set about fixing the buckle in Craig's rear wheel. In no time at all, Craig is cruising along without a care in the world.

We arrive at La Crotoy to find every available restaurant is full and Craig's rear tyre is empty.

What!

Cathie buys take-away chips while I set about fixing Craig's tube yet again.

I carefully wheel him to the sea wall.

'You see that deep water, Craig,' I say, in a low menacing voice. 'That could be your resting place ...'

Craig meekly explains that Ferraris don't run on cheap tyres. I tell him he's no Ferrari. He responds that I'm no Sebastian Vettel.

Cathie returns with over-salted soggy chips and we eat a quiet lunch looking out at the very deep cold water of the bay. Craig doesn't say a word. I stare at his back tyre, daring it to deflate before my eyes.

It's a glorious bay of sailboats and seagulls, sandbars and salt marshes. This was where William the Conquerer marshalled his fleet. I believe they sailed to England with the cry of 'Bill the Bastard no more!'

The Somme is also forever connected with the mud, blood and sacrifice of so many young men in World War One. So much sadness amongst so much beauty.

We leave Le Crotoy to the holidaymakers. Craig's tyre is not pumped up as much as it should be, but I reason that a softer ride may cause less trouble. Craig smiles smugly and I promise him a new tyre if we make it to Berck without any more dramas. He says he'll think about it. I should have thrown him into the bay.

Our accommodation in Berck is in a suburban home owned by Brigitte, a lovely host who offers me and Cathie a beer on arrival and confirms that there is a velo shop just around the corner. I scull my beer and take Craig to the doctor, who promptly says there's nothing wrong with him. With limited French, I can't explain that the rear tyre has deteriorated by spending a winter cooped up in a cold and draughty barn. Doctor Velo shrugs and fits a new tyre. It's impossibly cheap and I fear not of the highest quality. Craig doesn't say a word. He's always hated doctors.

We return to our suburban sanctuary where Brigitte and Cathie are discussing dieting. My beautiful wife does not need to diet and loves food with a fury so I'm a little amused by this conversation. It seems Brigitte, an elegant and thin woman who wears clothes the way only a Frenchwoman can, runs a six-week diet regimen. She's a soul sister to Jenny Craig, the famous namesake of our bicycles who sells pre-fab meals to people worried about their calorie intake. I'd hoped such nonsense hadn't breached the fat-lined walls of France, but Brigitte assures us business is brisk. I pretend to be pleased for her. She's a lovely woman. I just don't agree with diets.

The only diet I've ever understood is the mantra of the famous American journalist, Michael Pollan who says we should, 'Eat food. Not too much. Mostly plants.' He also suggests we should only eat food that our Grandmother would recognise. This means butter instead of margarine, plain yoghurt over flavoured yoghurt, wholegrain bread rather than hi-fibre folate-added salt-reduced plastic bread. In short, avoid processed foods at all costs. It's simple and relatively easy to follow. But I can't explain this to Brigitte, who graciously agrees that the best diet is eighty-kilometres per day on Craig and Jenny.

We cycle down to the beach for dinner. Brigitte, despite her calorie-counting has recommended the best restaurant in Berck for this evening. Before dinner, we stroll along the foreshore. The wide sand beach, the sprawling old hospital complex, the gelato-coloured beach huts - it looks oddly familiar. I keep telling Cathie I've seen this place before. She suggests the lack of food is making me hallucinate.

I cast my eyes up to the hospital once more and then it hits me.

'The diving bell and the butterfly,' I shout, 'the movie!'

One of our favourite French films tells the tragic yet heroic tale of Jean-Dominique Bauby, the editor of a fashion magazine who suffers a massive stroke that leaves him with locked-in syndrome. This terrible condition means he cannot move any part of his body and yet his mental faculties remain unimpaired. In the movie and in real-life, he was cared for in this very hospital. Undaunted by this prison sentence, Jean-Dominique wrote about his condition and life. How you may ask? By what became known as *partner-assisted scanning*. As his assistant spoke each letter of the alphabet, she'd watch for Bauby to blink his left eyelid, the only part of his body that still moved. He wrote the book, literally one letter at a time.

The book was published in 1997 and went on to become a bestseller throughout Europe, spurning the movie in question. Sadly, Jean-Dominique Bauby died two days after its publication.

We cast one more glance up at the hospital and walk slowly along the foreshore to dinner. Is it churlish to admit that the food tasted much better knowing that a life, anyone's life, is to be treasured in all its small mercies?

Chapter Five

Nord-Pas-de-Calais, France

Despite talk of diets, Brigitte provides us with a breakfast of epic proportions. Neither of us can say no. Today's ride promises numerous hill climbs but begins with a calm cycle along the school bus route linking Berck with its suburbs. Thin healthy-looking French teenagers giggle and chat or listen to iPods at each bus stop - the boys awkward and slight, the girls with long hair and tight jeans. No-one wears a school uniform. I hate the way we dress our young adults in a strict code of shorts and long socks or billowing dresses, as if we're trying to punish them for being young and beautiful. In France, teenagers look happy and young, as they should.

Craig appears to be happier this morning, chugging away smoothly on his brand-new rear tyre. The D940 is flanked with turquoise street lamps which have garlands of flowers three metres above the footpath. The flowers cascade down. We're cycling through a flower tunnel.

Before Etaples, we stop at the Commonwealth war cemetery. We are alone except for the five workmen assiduously tending to the pristine gardens. Consecrated in May 1915, this site holds the beloved remains of over ten thousand Commonwealth men and women who sacrificed their lives along this stretch of coast line. The grass is wet with dew glistening in the morning light. The pale stone memorials look down over the hillside of simple gravestones - all that remains from four years of relentless trench warfare along the Western Front. The forest beyond masks the perfect blue of the Channel from where so many of these soldiers arrived. We wander in silence, each gravestone is set beside a flowering plant - row upon row of colour and stone, colour and stone. The sun filters through the trees and a fine mist like a lost breath rises from the ground.

North of Etaples we enter a forest and bump along a hard path of gravel. Boulogne-sur-Mer surely takes the prize as the easiest city to cycle through on a newly-developed waterfront that caters for cyclist and pedestrian and relegates cars to distant parking stations. A pleasure. We climb the first of many hills and look down over cargo ships crossing the Channel. A Mondrian-inspired apple sculpture takes pride of place at one roundabout. I nearly run off the road admiring its glossy size and shape.

We enter Wimereux, cycling past luxury holiday villas constructed of stained timber with extensive verandahs looking over the Channel. I recall this town is where the poet, John McCrae is buried. McCrae penned the achingly timeless 'In Flanders Fields' while fighting in nearby Ypres. He'd witnessed the death of his close friend, Alexis Helmer and performed the burial service where he noticed that poppies grew over the graves of fellow soldiers. So began his immortal first lines,

In Flanders fields the poppies blow
Between the crosses, row on row.

Wimereux is a quiet village of Belle Époque architecture and a well-manicured golf course. Many of the houses appear closed and shuttered for the season, a sure sign of being owned by people from Paris or Lille who use them only for summer vacations. Wimereux sleeps in the spring. We cycle up and down the nearby Dunes de Slack until Ambletuese. It's time for lunch and le Viking restaurant is open on the busy D940 but I have visions of a seaside restaurant looking over the Channel. So we plough down a hill to the waterfront where everything is closed. Perhaps Ambletuese is French for *ghost town*? There isn't even the obligatory old lady walking her dog along the promenade. The wind blows from the ocean and disturbs not a person. Everyone is bunkered down indoors or back up at le Viking. Which is where we head for beer and beef bourgignon.

We spend the afternoon climbing slowly up one windswept hill before barrelling down another, alternating between a teeth-grinding eight kilometres per hour to a buttock-clenching fifty kilometres per hour. At Wissant, a seaside village favoured as a holiday destination by Charles de Gaulle, we stop for an ice-cream to take our minds off the horrendous crosswinds threatening to pitch us under the wheels of a truck or into a water-logged ditch. Never has an ice-cream tasted so good.

'Only two big hills to go,' I offer.

'Hills or mountains,' Cathie counters.

'Somewhere between the two,' I compromise.

'Then that's where you'll find me,' Cathie answers, before stoically rising from her comfortable cafe chair and returning to Jenny.

'Half of it is downhill,' I suggest.

'You're not helping,' comes the pithy reply.

Cap Gris Nez - or Cape Grey Nose - is the closest point on the French mainland to England, although with the suffocating wind we have as much chance of seeing the white cliffs of Dover as climbing this monstrous hill without sweating. In the distance is Cap Blanc Nez, the barren chalky brother. The lack of vegetation only encourages the wind and after climbing for a half-an-hour with a gradient nudging 10%, I pull over at the top and nearly get blown off Craig. I rest him precariously against a farm post and wait for Cathie. Despite the wind, the incline, the long line of cars and trucks, my beautiful wife pedals triumphantly atop the cape.

'Bravo,' I shout, but my voice is lost in the tumult.

'I need food,' she answers.

I promise her delicacies beyond measure in Sangatte. She keeps pedalling, leading me into the quaint old town and directly to a boulangerie. Sometimes I think she has an in-built radar able to lead her to the nearest food within a hundred miles. I wish I had a similar ability for beer.

Later that evening, while loading my Garmin onto the computer, I note that most apps have disabled the 'goal setting' function for the Cape route because it's regarded as too hazardous to encourage we cyclists to race the clock. I was battling exhaustion, not a time trial.

Our hotel room offers glimpses of the Channel if we lean far enough out the window. Which is what I do as evening comes and the wind ceases. All is calm on the waterfront as a long line of hungry Englishmen and women wait for the only restaurant in town to open. We push and barge and scurry like hungry rats to any available table. The manners of some people! And look, we seem to have chosen the best table looking out at the lonely street of double-storey houses and prowling tomcats. I mean real cats, not randy French teenagers.

I have salmon with pear and Roquefort cheese sauce - sounds scary, tastes delicious. Cathie orders her default dish, a cherve chaud salad.

'You deserve more than a salad after today,' I say.

'It's goats cheese. Loads of fat and taste,' she smiles, 'And besides, I've just ordered a half-litre of wine.'

My wife. She knows just what to say.

In the morning, the mysterious orange ball rises once again into a cloudless sky and France is luxuriating in the longest unbroken chain of perfect days since they won the World Cup in 1998. We skip breakfast in the hotel, wheeling Craig and Jenny out from their overnight barn before setting a cracking pace to Calais. It's amazing what hunger can do for one's pedal strokes. We pull up at a restaurant in the main square and order petit dejeuner. The waiter explains that they don't have croissants, only baguettes. When he sees my look of horror, he suggests I go to the nearby boulangerie and I can eat them here on his sun-filled terrace. Such a kind man, I leave him a tip. And numerous flakes of croissant.

Fortified, we cycle down the main street with a quick spin around the elegant Hotel de Ville, a red-brick behemoth complete with clock tower and statues of naked Greek gods. In front of the town hall is Rodin's famous *Les Bourgeois de Calais*. The statues were originally placed on a high plinth in a park, against the wishes of the artist who wanted the figures to be much closer to the citizens. He preached the language of solidarity. The town elders ignored him. Eventually, in 1926 the sculpture was moved to its present location in the car park of the town hall. Not quite fulfilling Rodin's wishes, but at least the good burghers are closer to we hoi polloi than they once were.

It's an easy ride along the coast this morning, even though the dunes block our view of the Channel. We detour regularly to check the ocean is still there. Yep, hasn't moved much in the last hour. We also marvel at the number of RVs camped in the most desolate windswept places along the coast. Do they deliberately choose the most unappealing location to drop anchor? Beside a rubbish dump, along a mosquito-infested swamp, opposite a shuttered and derelict hotel. The RV usually has two bicycles strapped to the rear, covered in plastic. Inside one RV, I spy an overweight man listening to the radio while his wife boils the kettle. The wind rocks the van and the two pensioners look out across the expanse like prisoners in a tiny cell. I wonder if the bikes ever get used? They seem quite happy to watch the world go by. We cycle past with a wave and creaking of gears. Or creaking of knees.

On each prominent cliff, concrete World War Two bunkers slowly crumble among the weeds and wild flowers. We cycle past a high tower doing an excellent imitation of a certain landmark in Pisa. An absent-minded council has built a picnic table and chairs, thoughtfully placed just where the tower will land. It wouldn't make for a relaxing picnic lunch.

We're making such quick time today, I'm worried we'll arrive at

Dunkirk too early. We detour to Gravelines where a village market fills the main square with stalls pungent with cheese and saucisson. A van sells glistening fresh seafood and a strawberry farmer has set up a rickety table near the Le Central bar. He's drawn a crude map showing how close to Gravelines his strawberry farm is located. With food that local, how can we resist. The berries are sensational.

Not so the advice we're given by the pretty girl in the Tourist Office. She suggests instead of battling the busy roads into Dunkirk, we should head inland to Bourbourg where we'll find a *canal beau* that will lead us right into the centre of the historic port. We naively set out along a path towards Bourbourg, picking our way through wetlands scattered with bird-hides and criss-crossed with noisy freeways before eventually finding Bourbourg, lonely and desolate on the flatland. The canal has no discernible path running alongside it. We take to the D-road, hoping to locate the much-vaunted path.

Non.

Thirty kilometres of cursing and truck-dodging in search of the cold stone heart of Dunkirk. Lunch is a baguette and cheese beside the canal, next to a graffiti-stained bus shelter. Along the road are disused industrial buildings, buildings about to be disused and fading signs announcing the sale of the disused. There appears to be more graffiti artists than willing buyers.

To cheer ourselves up, on arrival in Dunkirk we enter a glass-enclosed modern shopping centre and buy a water bottle for Jenny, a pair of knicks for myself and even splash out on the spare tyre for Craig. I just don't trust the one I bought yesterday. On the waterfront we eat an oversized coffee ice-cream at an outdoor restaurant.

At precisely the appointed hour, our host Annie arrives to show us the apartment we've booked for tonight. Up a winding tight staircase, it's light-filled and spacious. It even has a washing machine. Ten seconds after Annie leaves us, we both strip naked and toss all our clothes into the machine. Cathie showers and I wander the cool timber-floor apartment *au natural*. I wave at the gentleman in the opposite flat. He draws his curtains. The nerve of some people!

It's precisely fourteen days or forty-one meals since we've had the pleasure of cooking for ourselves. Suitably scrubbed and dressed, we head to the supermarket for eggs, cheese and half-a-dozen bottles of beer and a bottle of wine. Tonight we celebrate our last evening in France with a brie omelette and crusty baguette. With the windows open to catch the breeze off the Channel, I cannot think of a better way to end our blessed time in this country of dreams.

I fall asleep on the lounge clutching my fourth bottle of beer. Cathie's wine bottle lies empty on the floor. My wife lies full beside it.

Chapter Six

Belgium

We wake earlier than should be expected after so much food and drink. The leftover beer awaits the next lucky guest at Annie's place. We cycle along the foreshore. Dunkirk struggles to rouse itself this early. It's a splendid little town of seaside houses and yellow and green beach huts.

Two boys play football in a back alley, a cat watches the game from a first-floor window and we bid farewell to France.

On the French-Belgium border lies a small war cemetery. The graves of French soldiers are topped with a white cross while the British warriors lay under simple stone. The Tunisians who fought here on the side of the Allies are buried under more elaborate carved stone memorials. Each lists the name of the soldier, his regiment, the date of his death and the words 'Mort Pour La France.'

Our first sight of Belgium is the rising sun and a row of plain stocky brown houses. Cathie remarks that the windows seem smaller, the house more insular. I nod. We've been to Belgium before and I'm forever intrigued by the subtle differences between this small country and its neighbours France and The Netherlands. I openly admit I am yet to understand the folk who live in this flat land. They appear less courteous and friendly than the French and they're certainly much more restrained and insular than the ebullient Dutch. They are a mystery I hope to solve on this, our third brief visit.

We join bike lane number 65 that leads us into wealthy La Panne. The bike signs don't tell us where we are, or where we're heading, but we figure 65 sounds like a friendly number. La Panne is littered with ritzy cafes bulging with Belgians eating cream-covered cakes and drinking mugs of coffee. We follow a looping main street through the heart of town to the waterfront where numerous recent developments have noticeably elevated the skyline. Everyone wants a beach view, it seems.

At Sint Idesbald, we buy a *bouquet royal,* a rather prissy name for a custard and chocolate cake of doorstop proportions. We sit on a bollard and share it. The cafe dwellers all stare at us suspiciously. Perhaps eating cake in public is frowned upon? Although they're doing the same thing, albeit with the aid of a table, chairs, plate and fork.

Fingers will suffice for my wife and I. Tired of the sullen glances, we enter a cafe and order two coffees. The barista burns my milk beyond recognition. I return the coffee immediately. He shrugs. I don't know how to complain other than to say in faltering English, 'I'm sorry, it's burnt.' He does not understand.

Cathie, being a more generous soul suffers through the mug of torture. When I go to pay, I discover the owner speaks perfect English and doesn't much care for my opinion of his coffee-making skills and that'll be five euro, thanks. All I can say is if you're in Sint Idesbald, *l'Artisan Cafe* is not run by a true artist.

We continue to follow route 65 as it leads us on a convoluted dance through housing estates of immaculate gardens and pristine villas. At Nieuwpoort, recently erected three-storey wooden apartments face the canal across an expanse of garden large enough for ten football fields. We say hello to every cyclist we pass. Few respond. Some feign surprise that we've spoken. It's all very odd. If my lycra shorts had a zipper, I'd be wondering if it was undone such is the look of horror that befalls any Belgian I greet with a cheery 'bonjour.' The promenade at Neiuwpoort reeks of self-satisfied wealth. Clothing stores jostle for space alongside elegant cafes and restaurants. It feels as if I'm cycling through a catalogue for the latest gated community. Lots of people are out on bicycles. No-one smiles.

It's doing my head in.

I turn to my wife and open my mouth wide.

'Have I got something caught between my teeth,' I ask.

She smiles. She knows exactly what I mean.

To top things off, Craig gets a puncture. The new tyre lasted less than two days. I repair it while threatening to throw Craig in the canal if he so much as mentions the word Ferrari. Despite being passed by numerous cyclists, no-one stops to offer assistance. After I've pumped up the tube, I jump on Craig and mutter to myself, 'How far to the Dutch border.'

And then we get lost. Route 65 signs disappear as quickly as a comedy club in Brussels and we're left beside a long straight canal, wondering who to ask for directions. Eventually, one kind soul stops and offers help. We should turn left up ahead and follow route 11 into Ostend.

We cycle past a vast solar and wind-turbine farm. Four turbines do their slow arm-rolling action in the ocean breeze and I think of my country where we have twice as much sun and half as many brains. At distant Middelkerke, ugly eight-storey apartments block the view of the beach and cast shadows for eternity while we follow the circular and turgid route 11 through the industrial outskirts of Ostend. Oh, that wasn't the industrial outskirts. That was downtown Ostend.

Famished, we seek refuge in a restaurant on the main street. At three different tables, a single middle-aged lady dines alone. Each of the ladies in question wears glasses and looks like the type who keeps cats. At a fourth table, a man in his thirties dressed in a beige shirt and blue tie reads a science-fiction novel. In this restaurant of broken dreams, we pay top dollar for a reheated pasta dish that fills us but doesn't satisfy. I'm beginning to understand why no-one smiles.

I ask for a carafe of water. The waitress shakes her head. They do not give away water. We must buy expensive imported French mineral bubbly. I pass. I also somehow forget to leave a tip. The three ladies munch silently and stare into the distance.

The bike paths are crowded with cyclists in the early afternoon. It's difficult to describe the typical Belgian cyclist - they range from middle-aged couples (he's dressed in sailing shoes and slacks, she's wearing 3/4 length pants and a peach-coloured blouse) to lycra-wearing pelotons of young men in matching green jerseys to old guys riding bicycles that were the height of fashion in 1964. Quite a few have cards attached to their handlebars as if they're playing a curious game of bicycle-bingo. It eventually dawns on me that these are the route numbers they've decided on pre-ride.

Belgians don't get lost. That is left to more uncivilised races such as Australians who dig up shiploads of carbon-emitting coal and sell it at inflated prices to the Chinese when they could just as easily be harnessing all that sunshine and wind and tidal power for the betterment of humankind. We don't deserve free water!

We pass signs for Route numbers 4, 8, 5, 32, and 34. I have no idea where any of them lead. Fearing permanent mental paralysis, I choose route number 4 and hope for the best. We struggle along a waterfront road overlooking a beach where the locals are sand-whipped as they gaze out to sea and eat ice-cream. Finally, more by chance then logical endeavour we arrive in Blankenberge and celebrate by entering a swanky cafe with piles of cushions scattered over long bench seats. I contemplate reclining and asking my wife to feed me grapes, but instead order two waffles and a coffee.

The waffles are mind-bogglingly delicious. I instantly forgive the Belgians their sullen disposition as I spoon another tasty morsel into my mouth. Cathie has already finished her waffle and is contemplating ordering another. Even the coffee is excellent. And the waitress smiles as she asks if there's anything else we'd like. It's all I can do to resist requesting the recipe. We have found the secret to Belgium and it resides in a sweet little pastry of flour, sugar, milk, butter and yeast.

This unbridled joy lasts as long as it takes to cycle to our hotel just around the corner. The front door is locked. An envelope with our key is hidden in a security device. The code for this device beeps on my mobile phone just as I begin hurling a volley of abuse at the door.

We wheel Craig and Jenny through the deserted lobby. The adjoining restaurant is closed and has been for some time. The hotel does not offer dinner or breakfast. Or a receptionist to smilingly issue me with another pillow. I make do with the blanket. Our view extends over apartment rooftops cluttered with television antennas and chimney stacks.

In the evening, every restaurant along the foreshore is crowded. Most people seem to be eating steak and chips. I recall our last visit to this country where a man in a bar in Ghent told us that Belgians created the best waffles, beer and chips. He has been proven correct with the waffles and I enjoy a cold Stella Artois as much as the next man. So now it appears we must take the 'chip-challenge.'

The Taverne Dame Blanche offers Belgian beer as cheap as chips and err ... chips, accompanied by a mixed grill of all the usual suspects. The beer is great, the meat tasteless and covered in a pepper sauce that is neither creamy or peppery. The chips? They are ... adequate. Look, I didn't really expect great things from a Belgian meal, so I can't judge it too harshly. Indeed all the locals seem quite content eating chips and drinking beer, so who am I to complain. Unfortunately, the restaurant doesn't offer waffles for dessert.

In my experience, it is wise for the traveller to avoid all hotels with the words 'value' or 'budget' in their name. This is proven correct yet again at the Value-Stay Hotel in Blankenberge. The walls are thin, the bed hard, the wifi slow. This is the future of hotels where you book online and are greeted not by a smiling human at reception but by a security code and the faint smell of disinfectant. We sleep fitfully.

In the morning, there is indeed a woman at reception. To my utter embarrassment, I am rude to her within a few minutes. As we load the panniers on Craig and Jenny in the foyer, the woman asks if we have signed and dated the form that accompanied our security code. I admit I did not even notice such a form. She demands I go to my fourth-floor room to find it, fill it out and return it post haste.

I refuse.

She looks a little flustered and says it is a rule. I must.

I calmly suggest she print out the form and I'll be happy to fill it in. She can even have my autograph for free. She says that is not possible.

I shrug with the nonchalant air of someone who doesn't have a care in the world. No Frenchman could have shrugged as well as I. For one brief moment in Blankenberge, I am the Eric Cantona of shrug. I am so pleased with myself I offer an *shrug encore*. I'm sure I can hear applause coming from the dusty and empty hotel restaurant. I wheel Craig out of the front door and vow never to reside in another hotel that offers value such as this.

We cycle around the corner and pull up outside the first available bakery. The fruit croissants taste sweeter than usual and power us all the way to Zeebrugge harbour where a trolley line of freight cranes move between loads with all the grace of herons picking through a muddy riverbank.

Knokke-Heist is perhaps an unusual name for a beachside town, but it tries extremely hard to live up to its location by having numerous 'beach clubs' where luxurious outdoor furniture is flanked by ornamental palm trees or blue Buddhas or figurine swans. All manner of inappropriate beach themes are offered in a vain attempt to draw customers into the enclosure to drink overpriced Stella and be whipped by winds blowing off the coast. I'm so involved in checking out the latest silly beach theme that I almost fail to notice the eight-storey high-rise developments strung along the promenade. These disasters make the beach clubs seem positively restrained in their civility and charm.

From the nouveaux-riche to the filthy rich, we cycle past lovely stone mansions further along the beach. We reach a small hill and the end of the concrete path. There are no signs. A smiling man out for a morning jog nods hello. I quickly chase him on Craig and ask if he knows where we are.

'You are on top of a hill with one of the best views in all of Belgium,' he says, wiping his brow and gesturing out to sea with one arm.

I look out across the Channel. Two cargo ships are visible through the haze. On the beachside is an endless scrubland.

'We want to go to The Netherlands,' I ask, hoping he won't be offended.

'No problem, follow me,' he says. He leads me back along the path and points down a narrow dirt track.

'Follow this, first left, keep going for a few kilometres until you see a campground on your right,' he pauses for effect, 'And there is your destination.'

He smiles and sets off back down the promenade, waving and once again looking at one of the best views in all of Belgium. We set off along the track and soon enough come upon a sign announcing the way to the 'International Dyke.' A woman with very pale skin and wispy hair in a ponytail jogs towards us. She stops beside us and asks where we've cycled from.

'Blankenberge,' I say.

'But where did you start?' she asks.

'St Malo, in France,' I answer. She's a very friendly woman.

'Wonderful! And where do plan to complete this epic cycle,' she laughs.

'Umm, Prague, we hope,' I'm always nervous about mentioning a destination, as if saying the word will put a hoax on our trip.

She begins jogging on the spot to keep warm.

'I wish you good luck,' she says, before running towards Belgium.

Cathie and I stare at each other for a few seconds. It's the longest conversation we've had with anyone since entering Belgium.

'Maybe we're in The Netherlands,' I suggest.

Cathie nods, 'We must be.'

We cycle for a few kilometres before we arrive at a town with a very large dyke and a sign pointing to the ocean which says simply, 'Nordzee.'

We are in The Netherlands.

This is confirmed when we enter a bakery and the three women behind the counter all smile and greet us warmly. The eldest one draws rank and serves us. We can't speak Dutch but point at a large sticky cinnamon-topped bun. I order two of these and coffees. The woman reverts to English and suggests we take a seat in the sunny courtyard and she'll bring them out. I can't stop thinking how attractive these people are because they are smiling. I smile back. The world tilts ever so slightly on its axis.

It's Sunday morning and although the wind is pitching off the sea, the streets are full of people riding bicycles. The town has two bicycle shops and both are open. The cinnamon scroll tastes delicious, reminding me of the bulla cakes we had in Sweden years ago. Cathie's favourite. My wife reaches across and touches my hand, 'Thank you for leading me to The Netherlands.'

We both giggle. A weight lifts from our shoulders. Another weight begins to form around our stomachs as I order two more scrolls from the smiling trio. It's celebration time. We follow the dyke all the way to the ferry terminal where a boat leaves for the opposite shore in ten minutes. The only passengers are twenty cyclists. We ride on board and park our bikes in rows on the bottom deck. This ferry only takes pedestrians and bikes, not cars.

It's a smooth sail across the harbour and we're greeted in Vlissingen with the site of an wooden Dutch windmill slowly turning in front of a tall glass skyscraper. The old and the new and I know which one I prefer. At the train station, I stop to snap a photo of the car park. There are five cars parked in a single row. Next to them are perhaps two hundred bicycles overflowing onto the footpath from the available racks. I'm staggered by the number. On a Sunday! What must it be like on Monday when all the commuters head to work?

We cycle across a canal and I snap yet another photo of the long line of bridges down this waterway. They all lift up to let tall boats pass safely underneath. I've entered a country that understands how to move objects and people around in an orderly fashion. There is a bike path all the way to our destination for the evening.

Middelburg is a lovely medieval city in Zeeland, a province that for centuries has battled the sea, building ever more elaborate dykes and canals to prevent flooding, while profiting from the ocean's bounty. The expertise of the Dutch will be needed around the world when climate change brings ever-increasing storm surges and sea rises. Those of us in low-lying regions will be looking to the Dutch to solve a problem we're too preoccupied to fix in the dangerous present.

But enough talk of death and destruction. It's time for lunch. The first cafe we see has tables outside in the sun but we decide to step inside where the decor is wood panel, gold-braid mirrors and large comfortable booths. A friendly waitress in a crisp white blouse and black skirt takes our order of a club sandwich and a goats cheese salad. We clink beer bottles together and welcome each other to The Netherlands.

We drink and eat and clock watch until it's time to risk checking in early to our B&B, which is located down one of the most beautiful and historic streets of the old town. Imposing three-storey houses close in on the narrow alley. They all have large windows and an underground hatch to the basement. I wonder what they store down there? I tentatively knock on the black front door of our B&B. I'm greeted by Sam, the owner who skips down the stairs and opens the hatch, helping me carry Craig and Jenny to their underground garage. It's full of bottles of wine. I pat Craig's seat and tell him to keep his hands to himself. Sam shows us upstairs to our front room. It's large and airy with sunshine streaming through the windows. Sam explains that he's a flight steward and leaves for Hong Kong tonight, so his partner Simon will look after us. I ask him if he ever gets jet lag. He smiles and says, 'only after flying.'

We get dressed into more suitable Sunday clothes and wander the streets. There are no cars about, only pedestrians and people on bikes. While the city dates back to the 8th century, much of Middelburg was wiped out by German bombing raids in 1940. The Dutch have gone to great lengths to recreate the medieval character of the town amongst the few remaining truly old buildings. It's a superb recreation. The 12th century Abbey has been converted into a museum and its clock tower, nicknamed Lange Jan (tall John), remains to give a focal point to the old village. Today, the abbey is surrounded by a bewildering assortment of antique motorcycles. Triumphs, BSA, Moto Guzzi - some are even as old as their owners who all wear leather jackets, black jeans and grey beards as they drink beer and gaze lovingly towards their mechanical steeds.

We eat a punnet of strawberries on a bench seat in the square and try to choose in which outdoor cafe we'll drink beer. In the end, we play eeny-meeny-miny-moe and choose the one with the cheapest beer. At an appointed time, all the motorcyclists hop on their beloved bikes and start their motors. The roar is akin to a jet fighter landing in the town square. Having achieved maximum effect, they one-by-one circle the square and gun their machines down the narrow cobblestone lane leading out of town. After they've gone, a swarm of sparrows land on the street, looking for crumbs.

We have no idea what a typical Dutch meal is and unfortunately won't be able to find out tonight as the only restaurants open on the square are either Greek or Chinese. We choose Greek. Walking home in the evening, we pass lavish merchant stores from the 19th century. I try to detect whether they are a recreation or an original, but can't. No matter. They are beautiful.

Chapter Seven

Zeeland, The Netherlands

This morning, Simon offers us four choices of bread, eggs, ham, cheese, muesli, berries, freshly-squeezed orange juice and even a Dutch newspaper should I like to look at the pictures. This extravagance is served in a grand dining room with tall windows and heavy curtains. I feel almost regal, except I'm wearing lycra.

Craig has spent the night among rows of wine and spirits and I don't trust him to steer a straight line this morning. We set off nervously, having never cycled among so many people before. All of Middelburg is commuting on two wheels. It's not errant truck drivers we must watch out for, but zipping students on oversized black sit-up Dutch bikes built for cobblestones and wide paths. It's quite exciting being in the majority for a change, swept along in a two-wheeled tide. We quickly realise we can't just stop to check the iPad map whenever we want. We must give hand signals. We are now part of the traffic, not just aimless cyclists.

Eventually we shake the commuter belt and follow a path through paddocks of horses grazing on the lush green grass. A new country means a new number system for bike paths and we soon find ourselves heading west when I'm sure we should be going east. The landscape changes from fields to factories and the bike signs disappear. We backtrack a few kilometres and find the correct path. LF13A is the magical number to follow if we want to reach Germany not backtrack to France.

It's hard to describe the wonderful sense of liberation and excitement engendered by cycling into a new country. Everything looks different, from the excess of hydrangeas in the garden beds to the beauty of espalier decorating numerous front yards. The road surface appears smoother, there are more cows, farmers wave from their tractors and I stop at the entrance to an apple orchard and buy a bag of apples for the princely sum of one euro. They are crisp and juicy and we spend the morning smiling inanely at each other.

We have been to The Netherlands before. I'm fortunate to have a Dutch publisher for many of my young adult novels and they've been genial hosts on previous occasions in Amsterdam and Rotterdam, arranging school visits and media interviews for me, booking us into swank hotels and taking us to expensive restaurants as if I'm their most important author. I know they're being excessively charitable, but it's how I've come to view the Dutch - friendly, courteous and always willing to go that extra step to make a visitor feel welcome. They are a tall, handsome and happy people. And they grow delicious apples.

At the curiously named village of 's-Gravenpolder, we buy bread rolls and Gouda cheese before sitting in a park under an oak tree to eat lunch. All the children ride home from school. There are bicycles everywhere - old ladies go shopping on them, filling the handlebar basket with groceries, children as young as five ride without helmets or parental guidance, younger children are pulled in trailers behind sturdy bikes, there's even a sack-like contraption for mothers to carry babies while cycling. It gives the town a much more human scale and dimension. Everything moves at a pace we humans can understand. There are few cars and those that come into this village slow to a suitably gentle pace. We eat lunch, both thinking we've entered our type of country. I can't help but smile. When we hop back on Craig and Jenny I notice we are the only people wearing helmets. Safety is about infrastructure and prevention, not trying to limit the damage after the event.

For the first time on our journey we have started cycling two abreast as our default option. We chat about the canals, the paddocks of lush grass, the ripe smell of dairy cows, what we'll eat for lunch and dinner, which country makes the best cakes, why Lionel Messi is better than Christiano Ronaldo. Oh okay, I talk about that last topic. Cathie listens, vaguely.

At Hansweet - lovely name for a town - we cycle atop a levee. The sunshine off the water is almost blinding. A slow freighter ploughs through the channel and in the distance a row of windmills turn in synchronised harmony. We speed off the levee into the village and meet a cafe owner as friendly and serene as the town name. He's tall and skinny with cream trousers and a grey striped shirt. When he learns we're heading to Prague, he tells us of his last holiday in the fair city. His eyes get that faraway distracted look of wanderlust. When we leave he comes out from behind the counter and waves us away, watching as we climb back onto the dyke. I wonder if pre-determinism works with town names as much as names we give our children. Call a boy Jack and he'll be strong, reliable, independent. Call a boy Algernon and ...

We soon arrive at a complex lock where we join another couple waiting for the closest lock to fill before the drawbridge lowers and allows us to cross. Barges inhabit adjacent locks, heading in opposite directions and we cyclists plot a course around and over them. All operated with maximum efficiency by one worker in the lock tower. We have deliberately chosen a zig-zag route across Zeeland so we can experience more canals and locks and dykes and apple orchards in this cycling wonderland.

Yerseke is a small village on the shore of the Eastern Scheldt estuary. Our accommodation tonight is in a renovated Catholic church which has operated as a B&B for the past ten years. The owner, Meinte proudly shows us around his handiwork, outlining plans for an upper level where the community can hold meetings and parties. He has thoughtfully hung a sign on our door - Steven and Princess Cathie - and indeed, treats us like honoured royalty for the length of our stay. I have yet to meet a more contented man.

Cathie and I walk around the village in the late afternoon. There are children everywhere. As we walk down a narrow alley, a young girl approaches us carrying a box. She starts speaking to we strangers in Dutch. I think she's selling Girl Guide cookies. We try to explain we don't speak Dutch. She smiles and waves goodbye. Later we see two young boys carrying a similar box. In a chemist, two other girls have just sold a packet of waffles to the old lady behind the counter who engages them in a long cheerful conversation.

Around the next corner, five children are playing soccer in the street. Not on the footpath, but in the middle of the street. To an Australian, this seems inherently dangerous. What about the traffic? We notice that each of these groups of children are not accompanied by parents. Other children are cycling solo, or in pairs, around the streets of the village. No-one on a bike is wearing a helmet.

The village is swarming with happy children at play. Cars drive slowly along the streets and adults ride bicycles on errands. But no-one is looking after the children. They are joyously liberatingly happily free. Cathie and I order a beer at an outdoor cafe and watch the life of the village unfold.

I begin to notice certain design features of the village. We are sitting at a table perhaps one metre from the street and yet there is no gutter to delineate between footpath and roadway. The street is paved with bricks which serve to noticeably slow the traffic. Motorists, obviously aware that their 'space' is shared with pedestrians and cyclists, react accordingly, slowing to between 10 and 20 kph. The noise of car tyres on the paving stones means that everyone knows when a vehicle is approaching. And yet, no-one on a bike swerves towards the (non-existent) gutter. They just happily continue on their way, at about the same pace as the car. In such a shared space, it seems as if the natural goodness of we humans takes over - it isn't the biggest object that has precedence but the smallest, the most fragile.

This village is for people, not cars.

This village is for children. They live in a community which cares about their safety, not by locking them behind closed doors to play with a computer or by transporting them to afternoon sports in a four-wheel-drive, but by creating an environment where the whole village is their playground - from the street to the waterfront.

It reminds us both of our childhood, when after school was a time to run wild, play with your mates and to have adventures. Where the bicycle is the vehicle for the endless possibilities of the afternoon.

For dinner, Meinte has booked us a table at the cheapest restaurant in town, a seafood shanty overlooking the marina called De Viskeete. We're offered the best seat in the house in the corner of the enclosed verandah. We can watch the boats come in from the estuary while we eat fish stew. The waitress takes extra care to check we have everything we need. Even though she can't speak English, she keeps a watchful eye on our water (yes, it's free) and bread basket. I think Meinte has used his influence on our behalf.

At the table next to us sit two very old men. I'm sure they're brothers. They could be twins. Both are perhaps ninety years old and have bald heads marked with numerous sunspots from a life at sea, I imagine. Their hands are incredibly wrinkled and their movements slow yet precise. I envision them eating here once a week, with each brother taking turns to sit at the prime chair with the best view over the sea.

We walk home along the foreshore, past the numerous oyster and mussel farms. The smell of the ocean drifts across the town. In the square, workers in fluorescent tops mingle with men and women in business suits over a beer. Children continue to play football in the alley. We could live in a place like this.

Breakfast this morning is a weight-watcher's nightmare - the table is loaded with delicacies including twelve chocolate almonds, two handcrafted gift-wrapped chocolates and tiny cubes of cake. Meinte brings us coffee with his 'specially-frothed' milk, poured expertly from a saucepan. 'Just like my Mum used to do it,' he explains. He offers four types of bread in a basket as well as jams and cheese and salami. Meinte's wife Anna brings an even larger plate of cakes including a bulla. Cathie quickly snaffles that.

Their three daughters drop in to say hello. The youngest, Emma who is eight keeps looking at Cathie for perhaps longer than is usual. When she leaves, Meinte explains it's because she wondered what Australian royalty looks like. We'd forgotten the Princess Cathie sign on our door. But if Cathie's a princess, surely I can't be a prince? Perhaps I'm her servant.

Later while we're talking to Meinte in his kitchen, Emma prepares to leave for school. She kisses him and waves once from the back door. Then she goes into the garden to fetch her bicycle and waves again. Meinte quietly explains that they have a ritual each morning where she waves three times. He's confident Emma will wave after opening the back gate, just before hopping on her bike and cycling down the alley. Sure enough, she turns, smiles and waves. It's all I can do to stop from crying.

We pack Craig and Jenny and reluctantly leave this slice of heaven. Meinte and Anna come to the church entrance to say goodbye. As we cycle away, we turn not once, not twice, but three times to wave to these gentle kindly folk. Meinte can be heard laughing as we turn the corner and head west. A smart man knows that if you start each morning in such a positive and loving way, everything will look rosy, no matter what you encounter.

We cycle past fields of apples and pears, the trees laden with ripe fruit, bins stacked three high waiting to be filled. The farmers are out in tractors and they all seem to be smiling. My guess is the season has been very kind. Perhaps they wave to their daughters three times each morning before going into the fields?

After cycling along another dyke, we turn onto a road lined with plane trees offering shade from yet another sunny day. The ploughed soil looks like oversized blocks of dark chocolate scattered across the paddock. You could grow anything and everything in this rich expanse.

Last night I discovered a website which explained the intricacy of the Dutch bicycle system. I have jotted down my own version of bicycle-bingo. I'm calmly picking off the turns - yep, follow 54 until 48, then 67 until we reach Rillard. Easy once you know how.

We climb a short rise and find ourselves on a dyke facing a huge expanse of water. I had no idea we were that close to the sea. If not for the clever engineering of generations of Dutch, we'd by cycling under two metres of water. The typography is mercifully flat, the only climbing is up to the dykes. We see as many boats as we do cars. After Rillard, we cruise down to a huge bay where three small fishing boats wait at anchor. I look across the water but can't see land on the other side.

On previous visits to The Netherlands, we've driven between the major cities. I've thought of the country as endless transport infrastructure - highways and trucks and barges and rivers and airports. Ceaseless noise and energy. It was a land to get across, a noisy waypoint between the more scenic destinations of Denmark or Germany. Nothing but industry and cramped cities. It seemed you could not go anywhere in the country without being haunted by a highway.

On a bicycle in distant Zeeland, I realise how wrong I was. And how stupid assumptions made from the driver's seat of a car can be. The only sounds I hear now are the lapping of the tide on the foreshore and the chain slapping against the mast. A bicycle is the only way to see this gentle land.

'You hear that Craig, I'm pleased you're here,' I say.

Cathie smiles. 'You have forgiven him his sins?'

'For now,' I say.

We spy a number of road signs pointing in the direction of Bergen op Zoom, our destination for today, but steadfastly refuse to follow them because my bicycle-bingo advises we stick to route 31. We cycle through a dense forest of tall trees and creeping vines laced with walking paths and signs warning us to watch out for horses. The bike sign keeps assuring us that Bergen is three kilometres away and yet we cycle five kilometres through this silent and forest. Eventually, I ask two walkers for directions. The young woman with dark hair and a bandanna points down the road we're on and says breezily, 'it's 500 metres that way.'

Sure enough, at the end of the road, Bergen appears as if hatched from the forest floor. Which helps explains the origin of its unusual name. The city was built at a place where two types of soil meet: sandy and marine clay. The sandy soil pushed against the marine clay, forming hills over several centuries. *Bergen* in Dutch means hills while *Zoom* refers to the border where the hills were formed. The city also has a minor planet named after it. I like that, a planet with *Zoom* in the title.

We zoom into the city and are welcomed to our B&B by Alfred, a dapper man in a crisp white shirt, slim-fitting grey trousers and shiny black shoes. He leads us to our room, dubbed the 'Superior Suite' and for the next few minutes Cathie and I walk around in a speechless daze. The room is enormous with black leather chairs, a huge bed, an espresso machine underneath a large television screen and a very gay red and black artwork on the wall. The bathroom is almost as large as the bedroom and includes a spa bath, sauna and his and her 'beauty stations.' All this and breakfast for the price we'd pay for a fly-blown drive-through motel in a country town in Australia. Although we feel guilty indulging in such luxury, we keep reminding ourselves that this equates to standard accommodation rates in rural Australia.

In the afternoon, I sit in the back garden surrounded by neat box hedges listening to the fountain and eating complimentary chocolates because the scales in our bathroom indicate I have not gained any weight since leaving my home country. I know they're wrong, but who cares.

As the sun sets, we order beer and waffles from a cafe on the main square in town under the towering Gertrudiskerk, a Catholic church dating back to the 15th century. Alas, the Dutch can design brilliant bike paths but have yet to master the intricacies of the waffle. Too light, too sweet and not enough cream. It's a splendid square devoted to hotels, cafes and restaurants vying for our attention with window boxes of cascading flowers and large signs displaying all manner of roast meats and froth-topped glasses of beer. We circle the square twice, inspecting the menus like critics at an art exhibition. Too much of a flourish here, not enough substance there, he's just showing off with that feeble attempt at a post-modern chicken ... let's choose the roast pork with splashes of asparagus and new-season beans, my dear?

And so we do. It doesn't rival the best of Naples pizza or Paris canard, but for a whimsical Dutch pig, I can't wish for more succulence. What's that you say? Succulence isn't a word? Don't you know I was once Australia's most feared food critic? Oh okay, I wrote the odd review for a Sydney newspaper - one hundred words on budget restaurants. With such a limited range, one occasionally had to invent words.

Succulated, we return to our extravagant digs and fall asleep listening to the tinkle of the garden fountain and the bad language of the next door neighbour. Something to do with Ajax losing the football. I always thought Ajax was the name of a reputable dishwashing liquid.

Chapter Eight

Noord Brabant, The Netherlands

It's no surprise we dine on numerous extravagances at breakfast. I wonder how many breads are available in a typical Dutch bakery? Too many to consume in one sitting. It's a hazy morning of alluring mist. I'm a sucker for taking photos of trees like skeletal ghosts in the soft aura. Animals are framed by an impenetrable grey smudge as though the artist only bothered to paint the cow and left everything in the background indistinct. It's like looking at the world through vaseline eyelashes.

The roads are quiet, the fields rich with vegetables and a chestnut filly prances around the perimeter of a paddock, her mother content to munch on the lush grass.

Look away now, dear reader as I hereby apologise to the gentle corn farmer whose field I used as a toilet because the alternatives were too distant or too locked. I can mount a suitable argument about fertiliser, but perhaps a benign travel memoir is not the correct forum? Cathie cycled ahead slowly. Craig fell over. I'm sure it's because in the rush I didn't lean him against the post properly. He says he fell over from embarrassment. We hurriedly cycle away, vowing not to return to Wouwsche in the near future.

We enter a long stretch of forest, logs strewn alongside the gravel path. Our pace quickens noticeably when Cathie spots a sign indicating a fietscafe is two kilometres down the green tunnel. We love the concept of a cafe for walkers and cyclists. How very civilised. The Herberg Pannehuske dates from 1891 and is a lovely single-storey white stone building with a scatter of chairs and tables in the garden.

We assume *pannehuske* means *pancake house* so Cathie orders one with apple and cream. I give the Dutch waffle another chance. Soon after ordering, a group of four ladies arrive and immediately order the *house speciality* that we'd somehow missed on the menu - a huge slice of apple cake with enough cream to clog every artery in our body. They look fabulous. The cakes, I mean. Although, the ladies too look fabulously happy. Our pancakes and waffles? We'll order the *house speciality* next time.

I've begun to notice tiny 'personal' churches, often located on the corner of two lonely backroads. The small stone buildings, usually sheltered by a large tree contain a simple altar with a small statue of Jesus, a few candle-holders and a bench seat large enough to hold four pilgrims. They have no doors or windows, just an opening on one side. They are obviously still in use, with a well-swept tile floor and candles in each holder. It's like walking into a spiritual cave.

We follow a sandy track through a glorious forest of oak and pine trees with the smell of fresh-cut logs stacked in piles beside the path. The sand makes for fun riding. I almost 'come a cropper' but Craig, reliable steed that he is, rights himself just in time. He suggests I slow down. I answer it's time for lunch. We pass a green-tinged small lake with delicate sun rays filtering through the trees to the forest floor of orange leaves. Two old ladies sit on the only bench seat in the glade, chatting.

We eventually come to a bitumen road and I confidently follow the bicycle-bingo sign left. We pass two enticing restaurants and an imposing old building of brick, barbed-wire and turrets now housing a jail or Europe's most fortified house. It seems so out of place in this gentle forest.

We're entering the town of Breda which is not part of my bicycle-bingo. We're lost. I thought the Dutch-system was foolproof. Craig says something unkind about never having encountered a fool quite like me. I threaten to leave him outside the prison. Instead, we park both bikes in a rack at the Seven Hills Restaurant and have a sandwich and a beer while contemplating where to go. It's an ironic name for a restaurant. We haven't encountered any hills in The Netherlands yet.

Back on the bikes, we return to the forest path hoping to locate the correct signs. A elderly Dutch couple who look like they've stepped out of an advertisement for retirement homes ask me for directions. When they hear my accent telling them we're lost as well, the grey-haired man chuckles loudly. He tells us they're looking for a popular canal path. I tell him we're hoping to go anywhere but Breda or backwards. We join forces and cycle along a track heading vaguely east. Sure enough, we come to a lovely wooden bridge over the canal in question. They wave and turn right while we continue on the much longer and lonelier path. We celebrate by eating a apple. A man who surely wins the award as Europe's slowest jogger approaches. His clothes are drenched in sweat and yet he appears to be running in slow-motion. I've finished the apple before he passes. At the end of the path, shuffle man rests against a tree while we head deeper into the forest.

In the small town of Gilze we stop for apple cake and espresso served by the happiest man in Noord-Brabant. Although he can't speak English he communicates effusively while we scoff his delicious cake. I suspect he's the Mayor of Gilze and is excited to meet tourists from the other side of the world. He keeps saying the word 'Australia' among a stream of Dutch. He doesn't quite understand where we're heading, but recognises the word 'Germany.' He encourages me to follow him into his office. He logs onto the computer and types a few words. The screen lights up with the ten-day forecast for Frankfurt. He laughs heartily and points to a column of zeros, saying 'no slag.' Now I thought 'slag' meant cream, but in this case I'm confident he means 'rain.' I'm very happy to learn there will be no rain on our path through Germany, but also disappointed that cream will not be magically falling from the sky. It would have saved us a fortune in cafe stops. Our friend slaps me on the back and we return to my patient wife with the news that neither rain nor cream will be bothering us in the next two weeks.

As if to emphasise the storybook beauty of the Dutch back country we're cycling through, a chicken begins to cross the road ahead of us. She hears us coming and stops in the centre, looking for refuge on either side. She takes a few tentative steps back before scampering into the safety of the undergrowth.

'Why did the chicken cross the road, Craig?' I ask.

A rooster in a paddock cackles loudly in answer.

The road into Tilburg is lined with imposing houses framed by tall trees and neatly cultivated gardens. Number 321 Bredasweg boasts a stately turret and an imperious gate. I'm half-expecting the neighbour's house to be surrounded by a moat with access only over a drawbridge?

I'm very excited to be entering a town which hosts a 10-day funfair each year, with one day given over to gay celebrations, labelled 'Pink Monday.' How I love University towns. Everyone stays twenty-one years old except a few crusty old lecturers who wear tatty tweed jackets and corduroy trousers, their beards greying, hair thinning and their appetite for experimentation slowly diminishing with each advancing year. Eventually, they retire and are replaced by prematurely old forty-somethings wondering where all these young people came from.

Until the 1960s, Tilburg was considered the wool capital of The Netherlands with many fine old buildings including the classical city hall, registered as a National monument. But with a tidal wave of modernism flooding through the Mayor's office, this and many other old buildings were demolished to make way for car parks, skyscrapers and the usual grey brick tat. The Mayor in question, Cees Becht soon became known as Cees the Demolisher. Even today, five decades after his flat-earth reign, Tilburg appears a city without a heart. We cycle down streets of neon-light shops and through numerous featureless squares before being spat out near the train tracks, no wiser for our journey.

Our apartment is in a nondescript industrial area of car yards, service stations and furniture factories. The owner leads us up two flights of narrow winding stairs to a large space furnished in a garish 1980's style of white pine furniture. A flabby lounge of beige vinyl is framed by orange curtains on aluminium windows. In the bathroom is an oversized jacuzzi. We're so depressed by Tilburg we go to the supermarket and buy groceries for dinner, stocking up on chocolate and beer. That should help our mood.

This morning, we depart from tedious Tilburg as early as possible. I'm always impressed with the thoughtful details of Dutch cycling infrastructure - traffic lights give cyclists a head-start, bollards and kerbing protect us from vehicles and paths that, in most cases, seem to connect into a coherent whole. If only the Dutch didn't ride so quickly. Craig is shunted to the right of each path as little old ladies and long-haired University students alike thunder past. We retreat to a quiet backroad, past dairy farms and gardens in red rose bloom. The feits cafe on the outskirts of the unfortunately-named village of Spoordonk isn't open yet. A pity as it resides in a beautiful old horse barn of brown timber and heavy beams. The horses are banished to a nearby paddock.

We divert from the road to cross a large expanse of land that looks oddly like the Australian outback. A red dirt path snakes between brown spinifex-grass prairie. Low shrubby trees frame the horizon. It's so different from the lush green pastures we've been cycling past, I suspect the excess of jam and sugary cakes for breakfast this morning is causing hallucinations. I slap a large mosquito feasting on my arm and follow the deep four-wheel-drive tracks in the dirt. It's a curious sensation to be pushed back to an environment that seems so familiar and yet so far away. We expect a kangaroo to bound across our path at any moment.

Ten minutes later we're cycling past dairy cows and green paddocks and wondering what the hell that was all about? At Boxtel, there's too much industry and too many container terminals before we reach the town square and the sanity of apple cake and espresso. I check the photos in my camera - the dry grasslands, the red dirt, the stumpy trees. A little piece of Australia, captured in pixel harmony.

While we're sitting at the cafe, two men dressed in light-blue Council overalls remove a parking sign for disabled motorists from the square opposite. One man starts counting the bicycle spaces available, stepping carefully around Craig and Jenny. Two more officials arrive, dressed in grey trousers and white shirts. The four men enter a long and protracted discussion which, judging by the body language, appears to be about the acceptable ratio of disabled to bicycle parking stations. The men in overalls place the parking sign in the back of their truck and drive away. The two officials recount the bicycle parking stations. One writes the number in a notebook. They appear satisfied.

The theme of today's ride is how many cute animals we can cycle past. There's an endless number of pony farms east of Boxtel. The ponies stand in shaggy-headed bemusement looking across the fence line to the deer farm opposite, where newly born Bambis, sprightly and bright-eyed, wobble unsteadily next to their mothers.

We stop for lunch in a cafe adjoining a cow barn where five calves stare vacant-eyed at us as we eat toasted sandwiches and pray the wind doesn't change direction. I know what the consequence is for these calves, unfortunate enough to be born male on this dairy farm. Next to the cow barn is a small paddock of baby goats, bleating at one another in a plaintive refrain.

And now, dear reader, a simple question.

What are the first words a long-distance cyclist will learn in each new country they pass through, even though they'll never have to use those words in their daily travels?

A hint? Think capitalism.

Got it?

The answer is *for sale*.

Every few kilometres for the last two weeks, we've passed a sign announcing the house, farm or car is *Vendre* in French or *Te Koop* in Dutch. I only wish each sign would display the price. I quite like this simple two-storey farmhouse beside a canal near Zitjaart.

In the early afternoon, we arrive in Gemert as teenage students are leaving school. Behold the exodus of two hundred young people, all on bicycles as they swarm across the main road. The traffic is brought to a standstill.

Allow me to correct that last sentence.

Cars are brought to a stand still. These students on bicycles are the real *traffic* as they joyfully ride home. It's a perplexing site for Cathie and I who come from a country where the car is king and everyone else must cower in deference. These independent and happy young people seem oblivious as they cycle in between the motionless cars. The motorists wait until the cavalcade is over and unhurriedly go on their way. I believe the word I'm looking for is *civilisation*.

Four kilometres east of Gemert is a long tree-lined road where a very happy couple live in semi-retirement. Their names are Dick and Ans, both grey-haired and with skin weathered by prolonged exposure to the elements. They show us to our simple large room of sturdy wooden furniture, a long writing table and a double bed with a mosquito net. I've always loved mosquito nets on beds - it takes me back to my childhood sleeping on tropical verandahs safe and cosy under the mesh.

Ans asks if we'd like a drink. We both nod. Much clattering of cups and rattling of cutlery follows before we're ushered outdoors to a table set with a freshly-baked apple cake and coffee from a pot accompanied by huge dollops of fresh cream. It all tastes delicious. Dick and Ans tell us of their lives together, here among the sheep and goats and chickens and cats and dogs. Dick recalls his four years of farming in Norway and finding a very rare Mark Nine Jaguar motor vehicle. He talks lovingly of its beautiful lines and grand interior and how he bought it in 1970 just before he met Ans. She wasn't impressed by this petrol-guzzling monster, but Dick managed to charm her enough to let him keep the car. He turns towards the shed and winks. I know what's behind that door. He promises to show us after another slice of Ans's perfect apple cake.

An hour later, Dick opens the heavy driver's door and encourages me to get behind the wheel. I sit on the soft brown-leather seats behind the varnished steering wheel admiring the woodgrain dashboard and the elegant wing mirrors. Dick is not a car enthusiast - he's a lover of a beautiful timeless piece of machinery. He's conscious of recounting endless stories of this Jaguar, but can't resist one more tale of a friend who salvaged four side panels from somewhere in Asia. After freighting them back to Europe, he sold three for ten thousand euros apiece and the final one he gave to Dick. Dick rubs his hand along the panel, lovingly, devotedly.

Later, Ans talks just as enthusiastically about their farm and the animals, how they invite people with social or economic difficulties to spend time living here and working. These quiet gentle folk help to heal their visitors in body and soul until they love the place as much as the owners. We meet Victor, a refugee from the Balkans who came here years ago and has never left. He's a peaceful man who is slowly forgetting his traumatic past.

Before breakfast, we walk around the farm as the mist coats the grass in a glistening sheen. The gardens are awash with yellow, pink and red flowers. The dog sleeps in a corner of the barn, a horse eats wind-fallen apples and we prepare for the bounty of Ans's breakfast. We are not disappointed.

A few kilometres into today's ride we pass a large free-range chicken farm. Hundreds of birds peck and scratch in the grass looking for food. They carpet the field in joyful bundles of white. People opposed to free-range farming claim that chickens are too scared to roam outdoors and prefer to be cooped in barns. There's at least five hundred courageous dissenters among this healthy group. Ironically, further down the road we pass three large red buildings with blackened windows. Steam rises from the chimneys at either end. Huge feed vats are a tell-tale sign of what's inside. I cycle into the factory enclosure and try to peer through the window. It's opaque, but the smell of chicken shit is overpowering.

Apple tart and espresso help us forget the fortune - good or otherwise - of the animals we choose to eat. The cafe is located in a cartoon gallery set amid a large parkland of wild peet bogs. The owners offer guided tours through the landscape. As we're leaving, a group of middle-aged men walk out from the park. With trousers rolled above the knees, their feet and lower legs are black with mud and dirt. The men look as if they're eight-years-old again and have been told by their mothers to go and play in the mud.

After Deurne, we enter the magical De Peel peat region. Until recently, the precious fuel had been extracted from here since the Middle Ages. Numerous canals were dug to allow the barges access to the peat bogs. The border of Nord Brabaant and Limburg is a delightful maze of wetlands, canals and forest. For eight kilometres we cycle alongside one of these canals, marvelling at the green fronded water, the overhanging yellow and orange leafed trees, the shadows cast on the still water. I spend more time behind the camera lens than in the saddle. The canal is crossed by cute green-frame lifting bridges and I set Craig against the pylon for a photo. He's so captivated by the serenity that he doesn't grumble. For an hour, time stops. There's just us and the wonder of the canals.

In Helenaveen, we eat an omelette at a cafe with tables strung around the street corner. The church bells opposite toll for midday and I watch a man repair a bicycle tyre without swearing. He's also drinking a beer at the same time, so perhaps that lessens the anguish. His wife watches him while drinking a glass of wine and when he finishes, she orders him another beer as a reward. I look knowingly at Cathie. She smiles, 'all good things come ...'

We are now in the region of Limburg and today will be our final day in The Netherlands. We both want to come back and explore the rest of the low lands by bicycle. Limburg sits uncomfortably on the border with Germany and has recently undergone a transformation from industries focusing on peet extraction and coal mining to petrochemical production and tourism. I'm not quite sure how those two competing interests go together. Certainly, I'd be happy to wander the peet regions for days on end, but a guided tour through Chemelot Industrial Park? Maybe not. There are however numerous Limburg breweries to consider.

We cruise downhill to the Maas River, past a rather appealing hotel with a scatter of tables overlooking the stream. At the water's edge we wait for the ferry to take us across to where the twin spires of Sint-Martinus church dominates the town of Tegelen. We spend the afternoon looking for our guesthouse. We seek it high and low, along alley and highway, ask directions from shopkeepers and pedestrians, look at town maps and our iPad, all in vain. All because some stupid man hasn't written down the directions correctly. Eventually, we phone ahead and ask the owners. It's not actually in Tegelen. In fact, it's precisely one hundred and twenty metres from the German border on the main road four kilometres south of town. Oh well. It's a lovely ramshackle house run by a husband and wife team who happily show us to our large room on the second floor, with a window overlooking the garden and the shed where Craig and Jenny take a well-earned rest, having successfully transported us across our third European country.

However their work is not finished for the day. In the evening, we cycle back into town and across the river on the ferry to eat fish soup followed by steak and chips. And try some of that Limburgian beer.

Later in the evening, a large group of men arrive on bicycles. They take most of the outdoor tables and order gallons of golden brew. I think of my own country and our rather vain masculine ways. I can't imagine twenty men arriving at an Australian pub on bicycles to drink beer.

'I like The Netherlands very much,' I say.

'Cycling makes everything less aggressive,' says Cathie.

Indeed.

Chapter Nine:

North Rhine-Westphalia, Germany

Precisely fifty-five seconds after departing from our guesthouse this morning we enter Germany. The bike signs change from numbers to town names with helpful distance markers added. Danke! It's a cloudy morning which threatens rain from the north-east. We pass through the lovely border village of Kaldenkirchen where the present-day Amish and Mennonite communities of the USA can trace their ancestors.

The cycle path closely follows the B509 and it looks to be taking us straight up a rather daunting hill until we're rescued by a jovial man on a road bike. He tells us to follow him and winks, 'I know a back way.' He leads us at reliably slow pace along an overgrown forest path with a gentle incline. He's impressed when I tell him where we've cycled from and how every day we've had clear skies. He shakes his head ruefully, 'Not today, my friend. It will rain in one hour.' I look up, the clouds seem far away and not too bleak. I check my watch, it's 9:20 am. He leaves us in Grefrath. As he cycles away, I notice he has a rain jacket tucked into the rear pocket of his jersey.

We stop at Kempen for coffee and nussschnecke. No that's not a spelling error, just a tasty nutty cake with too many consonants for its own good. The cafe has a rather formal dining area where elegant waitresses with perfect make-up serve neatly-attired middle-aged guests and two embarrassed lycra-wearing Australians. Kempen is the start of an eleven million strong metropolis that takes in the major German cities of Dusseldorf, Cologne and Bonn and yet still has space for quaint villages and fields and farms and bicycle paths.

We leave the cafe at 10:15 am and the rain begins to fall. Always trust a German cyclist when he talks about the weather. We pull wet-weather gear from the bottom of our panniers and reluctantly prepare for the deluge. Today, I'm attempting to steer us towards the Rhine river where I hope we'll find a bicycle path that will lead us into Dusseldorf. Easier said than done. Despite checking our iPad map every few kilometres, the river remains elusive. Krefeld is a much bigger town than I expected. We struggle through endless wide streets of cars and trams and shops yet nowhere can we find a sign that leads us to the river. So we go to Osterach instead where everyone is dressed in marching band uniforms, carrying oversized tubas or trumpets and cymbals. There's a party happening somewhere. The rain has stopped. The lady in the bakery serves us a simple sandwich and as it's near closing time, she gives us free coffee. She's probably in a hurry to get to the party.

Confusingly, the bike signs all point towards Neuss, a small town across the river from Dusseldorf. No signs indicate the much bigger city. Looks like we're going to Neuss. We ramble through villages and fields and over underpasses and under overpasses. An hour later, we're in Neuss and Cathie is assigned the task of asking how to plot a route across river to Dusseldorf. Most people shake their heads and point vaguely east. A helpful man in a bike shop tells her that she should follow this road for one kilometre, turn left, locate the railway tracks and then ... good luck. It's apparent that every road into Dusseldorf is an autobahn not suitable for bikes. We pick our way through the wreckage of overgrown paths, bottle-strewn railway viaducts and pedestrian bridges. It's tedious and takes us another hour. Even when two cyclists give us directions, it's too complicated to follow. I need a beer!

Finally, we locate the Rhine. Incongruously, a flock of sheep graze in a paddock on the water's edge. Where the hell is Dusseldorf? Bouncing along a dirt path beside the Rhine, we come across a school of Sea Shepherd volunteers who direct us over a soaring new bicycle bridge with sublime views of the city skyline before landing us in the redeveloped foreshore. In a few minutes we've gone from desolate docklands to crowded markets. It's definitely time for a beer. And in Dusseldorf they drink *Altbier*, brewed using the time-proven method of warm-fermenting yeasts. So I try a glass. It's on the fruity side of lager and I like it very much. I order another and think of the past two weeks.

In that time, we have cycled from a country with towns named *Le-Mesnil-en-Vallee* and *Saint-Etienne-au-Mont* to a nation with towns called *Grevenbroich* and *Dusseldorf*; from the *Hotel de Ville* to the *Rathaus*; from caressing my vowels in saying *petit dejeuner* to spitting them out nasally when I ask for *fruhstuck*; from *wine* to *beer*; from the *pastoral* to the *industrial*; from *delicate-waisted mademoiselles* to *big-boned frauleins*; from *steak tartare* to *schnitzel*.

It's a truism that a visitor to any town is influenced by two things - the weather and the day on which they arrive. Dusseldorf puts on a sunny Saturday and crowds of smiling people flock the river's edge to eat and drink. A stream of scarf-wearing football fans sing through the square. By their clear-eyed optimism, I'd say they were heading to the game not drowning their post-match sorrows.

Dusseldorf is the sixth most populous city in Germany and home to a large Japanese community. The seminal German electronic band Kraftwerk began making drug-addled plink-plonk music here and the city is host to a bewildering number of museums and art galleries. As we cruise along well-designed paths, a protest march winds its way to the city square. The few police in attendance keep a respectful distance. I like Dusseldorf very much.

After checking into our hotel, we decide to risk choosing a tourist restaurant for dinner. The Brauerei Zum Schiffchen is the oldest restaurant in town, dating back to the early 17th century. It proudly lists Napoleon and Heinrich Heine as guests and claims to serve food prepared to the philosophy of the 12th century nun and healer Hildegard of Bingen. With all these boasts, I'm expecting exorbitant prices, churlish waiters and small servings.

An overweight waiter with a burgundy apron leads us to an outdoor table and asks if we'd like beer - there is no discussion which type of beer, of course. It's *Alt* or nothing. I'm happy with that. I order schweinehaxen and Cathie prefers rosti. Another waiter, who looks very much like Lurch from the American sit-com The Addams Family brings our food. I can't quite believe the size of the pork knuckle - it's as big as my head! I settle down to thirty minutes of crispy crackling, juicy meat, sauerkraut and potatoes - fat and salt and starch and I'll need another superb beer to wash it all down. Our original waiter is too busy laughing and chatting to guests to bother with us, but that's okay. There are enough waiters to go around. The bill is much smaller than the serving. It seems Hildegard knew her stuff.

We wander back to the hotel and the football fans are now cheering and singing in a much more off-key manner. Looks like they had a win. I should point out that an Australian plays for Fortuna Dusseldorf so how could they lose?

Rain should be outlawed on a Sunday. It's rather bleak outside and Craig doesn't help matters by having a gear-change tantrum. We slosh past opulent riverside apartment blocks and nod hello to the occasional dog walkers. Empty barges rush downstream while their counterparts sluggishly trundle up river. At Urdenbach, we board a punt for the short journey across river. As we cycle into Zons, the rain stops.

Zons is quite a surprise - a walled village with archeological sites from the 7th century, although much of the present town dates from the Middle Ages. Today there's a market. Stall holders sell home-made slate-roof birdhouses, silly hats and smooth river stones painted as fish. Plus that mainstay of the market - knitted doilies for the kitchen and bathroom. What is it about craft that turns many of us into dotty old ladies and grandfathers, searching for the kitsch and the unusable?

Ancient stone buildings stand uncomfortably beside dour brick houses, all surrounded by a historic wall. Medieval meets middle 1970s. We retreat to a homely cafe for German waffles with cream overload and a large pot of coffee. The beer tent is being erected in the square and the locals are getting into the spirit of festivities by dressing in medieval costumes. The dowdy weather will not prevent Zons from celebrating Sunday.

As we pass the huge Bayer chemical factory in Dormagen, Craig's front wheel gets caught in train tracks and I fall off in buffoonish slow motion, sliding along the gravel on my bottom - skinning my elbow, knee and thigh. Cathie rushes to my aid. I don't know if she can heal my wounded pride. The last time I fell off a bike, I was eleven years old. That's an unblemished record of forty-two years. Until now.

I can see the irony of having an accident in one of the safest countries in the world for riding a bike. Germany has a bewildering number of bike lanes, paths and forest tracks dedicated to two wheels. Can I blame the poor surface of this path for my misfortune? Or the rain? Or the wet leaves? Or just inattention on my part?

The answer is somewhere between my lack of focus - it happens after one thousand five hundred kilometres over twenty-one days - and the train tracks that redirected my front tyre. Yes, I know all about the dangers of train tracks on bitumen. Always ride across them at a 90 degree angle. Simple.

As I pick myself up from the wet path, I notice these tracks are angled confusingly at a slight bend in the path, so to approach them at the correct angle I had to illogically steer towards the fence. My addled brain didn't see the danger until I was ever so slowly falling to ground.

I pick up Craig and inspect the damage. I'm not sure if he's sniggering at my expense or whimpering in pain but he refuses to offer a choice of gears. Maybe this is his way of telling me to slow down. We limp into Cologne at a vastly reduced pace. I steer with one hand and contemplate whether my elbow has sustained more serious damage.

We locate the beautiful Cologne Cathedral immediately - it's the Gothic pile covered in scaffolding. What is it about major European landmarks that they spend much of their latter years surrounded by a meccano set of tubes and planks, with men in yellow hardhats pointing skywards as if blaming God for their engineering frustrations? The Cathedral is a monster with twin Gothic spires. It's difficult to get any perspective on the Cathedral because it's surrounded by roads. A caterpillar line of buses and hire cars ring the inner space. All this transport and movement detracts from the majesty of the 'building under repair.' It's still impressive, but when they get the 21st century out of the frame, it'll truly shine.

This town planning advice is from a man wearing torn lycra, bleeding from the knee and unable to straighten his elbow. Time to seek refuge in the Hotel Glockengasse located a few doors down from the original 4711 cologne shop, an elegant glass and polished wood shrine to perfume with the iconic 4711 bottles stacked five metres high. What is now a generic phrase for perfume - *eau de cologne* - originated on this street corner in the mid-18th century.

I've always thought the *water of Cologne* was a little too harsh and smelly to be labelled perfume. Do you know if you dial 4711 in Finland, you'll be put through to the poisons hotline? But then, the wonderful Audrey Hepburn as Holly Golightly in Breakfast at Tiffany's is also reputed to have used the magic spray. So who to trust?

The gentleman at hotel reception barely notices our muddy bicycles as we enter the foyer. In fact, he insists we leave them in the front room in full view of other guests. He says, 'they make a hotel look lived in.' I'm never going to hear the end of that from Craig on this trip. In our rear facing room on the second floor, I shower and take stock of my injuries. No major damage, just grazes and an elbow that refuses to lift above shoulder height or to straighten. Nothing a good cheesecake won't fix.

And Merzenich cafe near the Cathedral has just the lump to ease the pain, washed down with an excellent espresso. Cathie sits close and holds my good hand.

'You should see a doctor,' she says.

'And what if he told me to stop cycling for the next month,' I answer.

'That'll make Craig happy,' she smiles.

'Well, I'm not giving him that satisfaction!'

The sun comes out and we walk around the old town. In the centre of the square, not far from the Cathedral, there's a long line of people waiting to enter a circular tent that displays kaleidoscopic photographs of China.

Photos.

There's a ten-minute queue to look at advertising photographs.

And yet Cathie and I stroll into the sublime interior of the Cologne Cathedral without waiting. Give me the reputed resting place of the three wise men rather than a stack of *Visit China* scenes any day. I'm not quite sure how the wise men ended up in Germany's most visited landmark but whoever rests in the gold caskets certainly has a comfortable and expensive home. The triple sarcophagus is over one thousand years old and decorated with gold, silver and numerous jewels. It's considered the high point of Mosan art and is a shrine visited by many Christian pilgrims. We're suitably impressed and I learn that the relics of the Biblical Magi were given to the Archbishop of Cologne by the Holy Roman Emperor in 1164. Their presence lead to the building of this majestic cathedral to house the remains. The rest, as they say ... is a video clip in Uncle Stan's European Adventure.

We leave the three wise men and stare at the ninety-six bored men and women waiting in line to 'visit' China. Instead of a photographic tour of the far East, we choose a sunny cafe in the square and drink Kolsch beer, the local brew. My elbow is getting worse as the evening approaches. I suggest we search for a compact bandage first thing tomorrow. Tonight, we must eat!

Peter's Brauhaus has been serving kolsch beer since 1890 in its wood-panelled, lead-light window interior. It's only five in the afternoon, but everyone seems to be eating dinner so we hardly need convincing. I'm so distracted by the rudeness of the waitress that I end up ordering a mixed meat dish including blood sausage. I tentatively nibble a piece. It tastes like spicy soft flesh wrapped in cardboard. No worse than a dislocated elbow. I eat it all along with pork, smoked pork and speck. The kolsch is only served in 200 ml glasses which means I'm regularly hailing the rude waitress to ask for a refill. She gets more and more angry until she ignores me altogether. I can't work out what I've done to annoy her? She passes our table once more. I smile and point to our empty glasses. She snaps at me, 'I'm busy. You must wait.'

In my defence, she is not carrying any food or drink while walking past our table. How am I supposed to know when I can order a beer? Eventually, we're served. Cathie reckons the kolsch, being light and not too fizzy, needs to be served in small glasses to keep its optimum freshness. I reckon it's because this waitress likes being rude to as many people as possible, as often as possible. I leave her a tip the size of her charm.

We walk back to our hotel and I lie awake in bed wondering whether my elbow will be worse in the morning? I checked on Craig before coming upstairs. He's muddy and grumpy, but seems to have forgiven me for my wayward cycling.

In the morning, our ever-helpful host searches the internet for a shop in Bonn that will sell a compression support for my aching elbow. He shows me the location on Google before serving us an astonishingly good breakfast. If you're ever in Cologne, I can heartily recommend the Hotel Glockengasse.

The morning is cool and threatens rain. We're content to ride on a levee beside the Rhine, passing the ever-present barges and admiring the falling orange leaves. I'm cycling with one hand, my elbow is neither better or worse, just sore. I'm confident it'll improve over time.

Bonn is only twenty-five kilometres south of Cologne. We arrive as the shops are opening. Advertising signs are wheeled outdoors, tables layered with this season's specials and a long-haired young woman with pale make-up and high heels attaches a *50% off* sign to a trolley of dresses. In Bonngasse, a flurry of Japanese tourists have their photographs taken in front of a pink two-storey house with heavy dark green shutters. Welcome to the birthplace of Ludwig van Beethoven.

We celebrate the great man with a cherry pastry and espresso, followed by a visit to the specialist *bandagehaus*. In Australia, we can buy support bandages from any chemist. In Germany, I must visit a shop with a bewildering array of options. The friendly lady dressed in a white doctor's uniform introduces herself as Karin. I explain my injury and she rummages around under the counter before offering three choices, explaining the complexities of each option.

'Ah, which is the cheapest?' I ask.

Karin smiles and says, 'I'd recommend this one.' She holds up a flesh-coloured tube of bandage. 'Let's try a fitting, shall we.'

A fitting?

All the while, Karin talks to me about visiting Australia when she was young and the wonder of the outback. 'So much land, so dry and ... no people.'

An eye-watering thirty-two euros later, my elbow is caressed by a tight yet firm support as I wave goodbye to specialist Karin. In the market square a jovial man in a van sells bratwurst on a roll for two euros. We sit near the central fountain and admire the rococo style old town hall, built in 1737. I'm always impressed with the colour schemes of German public buildings. The old Bonn rathaus is a reserved pink and beige, topped with a gold crown above the doorway.

Bonn was the capital of West Germany before reunification, chosen because of its proximity to the powerhouse cities of Frankfurt and Cologne, yet small enough to not be seen as a serious rival. A political choice. I think of my own country where Canberra, our capital was constructed on a windswept sheep paddock because it was vaguely half-way between Melbourne and Sydney. Politicians are famous for wanting bland and land-locked cities as their residences. They don't like ports which are too bustling and open to the whims of change. And yet who in their right mind would choose Brasilia over Rio de Janeiro?

We continue along the Rhine where vineyards trace a line up the hills to old castles and ruins. There's a castle on every bend, keeping watch from its elevated vantage point, waiting for invaders from the East. We cruise past the multi-turreted whims of Konigswinter; the majestic white-washed Hotel Petersberg; and the 12th century ruins of Drachenfels, immortalised in verse by Byron, in painting by Hermann Hendrich and in legend with numerous tales of dragons and virgins and crusading knights. It's a suitably Gothic location for such tales, all the more so today as its wreathed in dark clouds.

'Why does the dragon always get slain,' I ask Cathie.

'Because good must conquer evil,' she says.

'Perhaps the dragon is just misunderstood,' I offer.

'Like Craig?'

'No, he's just ...'

'Whisper.'

'He's just ornery!' I shout, scaring the lady cyclist we're about to overtake.

At Ramagen, we stop for cheesecake and coffee. All that remains of the historic bridge is a mangle of iron and concrete. This was the scene of one of the decisive battles of the Second World War when the US Army 9th division secured the Rhine crossing. There's now a War Museum on both banks of the river.

I admire a town that hosts a three-day onion festival. We enter Bad Breisig to be greeted by hundreds of stalls lining the riverbank. They are selling everything but onions. The tat of modern markets is prominent - socks; hats and scarves; sugared almonds and assorted lollies; coffee pod machines; knives and scissors; brooms and baskets and a battalion of bratwurst and beer stalls.

We locate our B&B on the hill side of town. Our room is large and light and upon entering, I suggest we book it for an extra night. After three weeks of cycling, a rest day is in order. A chance to rest my throbbing elbow and celebrate onion weekend. We wander back to the Rhine and walk past every stall in town. Still no onions. The *Zwiebelmarkt*, held each year since 1374 is missing its star. Each year, Bad Breisig chooses a *Brunnenkonigin*, or 'Spa Queen' to represent the region. Perhaps they should have an 'Onion King?'

We eat dinner in a restaurant whose name I'm determined to remember because it was similar to a schmaltzy American pop singer from the 1960s. Cathie and I promptly forget the name once we return to the hotel. Cafe Sedaka? Cafe Diamond? Cafe Manilow? Cafe Como? My elbow hurt but not as much as my brain.

The next morning we rise early and dress in normal clothes. No lycra! We smile inanely at each other across the breakfast table. Craig and Jenny rest in a secure garage underneath the hotel as Cathie and I set out on a ferry across the Rhine to Bad Honnigen. It has an elegant single-turret schloss surrounded by vineyards pitching up the slope. And a cafe run by Italian immigrants who know how to make espresso. We sit at an outdoor table and contemplate doing nothing all day.

'Do you want to visit the schloss?' I ask.

'It's closed,' Cathie says.

'How do you know?'

'It's a private residence.'

'If I owned a 19th century castle, I'd let people visit,' I answer.

We order another coffee.

'We could walk along the Rhine,' I suggest.

'We'll cycle the same way tomorrow.'

'Or climb the hill above the vineyards,' I say.

Cathie doesn't even bother answering. In the end, we wander the quiet streets of Bad Honnigen before catching the ferry back to Bad Breisig. The ferryman speaks my language. The illiterate grunt. Our conversation went something like this.

'Zwae, bitte aahh der,' I ask.

'Zvie zvie uuhh,' he answers, pressing two tickets firmly into my hand.

Unable to find a stall offering German onion soup or fried onion rings, we decide on bratwurst on a roll and a local delicacy, potato cakes with apple sauce. *Delicacy* probably isn't the correct word, but it's delicious all the same.

While eating this brick of carbohydrate, I offer my beautiful wife a theory on food. It's ill-conceived and barely considered, like much of my musings. So let me share it with you. And remember, this theory comes from a man who has eaten almost non-stop from Saint Malo in France to the middle reaches of the Rhine river and only put on one kilo. Actually, it's not even a theory, more a simple question.

Is 'fast food' really 'fast food' when eaten in the country of origin?

While we in Australia may perceive pizza, sausage on a roll, fried rice, cevapi, burek and souvlaki as 'fast food' with all the negative connotations of being high in fat and 'bad for us,' why does it suddenly morph into a regional delicacy (hello potato cake!) when eaten beside the majestic Rhine river?

I've eaten pizza in Napoli that ranked in the Top Five meals of my life and yet I only paid a few dollars for it and many of the customers eat it every lunchtime of their lives. How does eating pizza in Napoli somehow give me immunity from the supposed effects of a poor diet and food choice, simply because it was eaten in the city of its origin?

Of course it doesn't. But I'd suggest it's because we in the West have such a contorted and twisted logic when it comes to food that we have taken much of the pleasure out of what we regularly put into our mouths and stomachs.

In short, fat isn't bad.

And nutrition as a 'science' is a load of rubbish. Folate and antioxidants are important but it's the food where they naturally occur that is the secret. Adding these nutrients after the fact won't solve our obesity epidemic.

It's not simply what we eat, it's how much we eat and whether we do anything between meals that really matters. There's a world of difference between a Napoli pizza eaten in a small family-run restaurant and a McCains Frozen Supreme reheated in the oven. Likewise, a bratwurst on a roll from a German stall to a packet of weiners bought from a supermarket. To use a well-worn cliche, 'it's the processing, stupid.' Or should I say, 'it's the processing, sugar.'

When it comes to our food choices, I'd prefer to trust in two things:
- the country of origin

- the person who produces it.

No, you don't have to move to Italy to eat good pizza, but it helps if the person who makes the pizza understands the basic tenets of how the country of origin produces the meal. That is, they appreciate and respect the ingredients that are used, the method of cooking and they produce it in a similar tradition.

If we continue to allow corporations to produce our food then it's the wrong food choice, no matter how much folate or antioxidants it contains.

Fortified with bratwurst and potato, we spend the afternoon wandering the markets, sampling the cakes before snoozing in our hotel room.

'Restaurant Anker,' I shout.

Cathie smiles. 'Paul Anka, of course.'

And so we return to the Restaurant Anker this evening. We're ridiculously early, but they serve Alt beer and I can't resist. The waiter tells us the menu isn't available for another hour, but my eagle-eyed wife has spied an old gentlemen tucking into bread and what we suspect is soup at a nearby table. We order two servings.

The waiter dutifully brings us a slice of dark bread and a bowl of apple sauce, not soup. We are confused. Do we spread the sauce on the bread? Or just spoon it into our mouths? I try the latter.

'It's a little ... underwhelming,' I venture.

'Potato cakes!' Cathie says.

'What?'

'The waiter will bring us potato cakes in a minute, you just wait,' she says.

Sure enough, a large plate of potato cakes, crisp on the outside, soft and salty on the inside arrives shortly. I wash this starchy miracle down with an Alt beer while Cathie chooses federweisser, a fizzy alcoholic fermented grape juice. I take a small sip. Then another large gulp. It's delicious. The secret to this brew is the yeast. Once added, the juice begins to ferment rapidly, with the sugars producing alcohol and carbon dioxide which gives it the refreshing sparkle. Cathie has found her beverage for the rest of the trip. After a few more glasses, we stagger home. I visit Craig in his garage. He's sound asleep, his handlebar touching Jenny's seat. She doesn't seem to mind.

Chapter Ten:

Rhineland, Germany

The morning brings high cloud and a crisp autumn breeze. Our expectations of an easy day cruising beside the Rhine are rudely shaken by a path that leads us away from the river and beside a noisy and tedious highway that takes us to Andernach, the birthplace of the legendary poet and barfly, Charles Bukowski. Perhaps appropriately, the first building we pass features a picture of a nude woman pole-dancing under a neon sign. Christina's Bar is located next to McDonald's and two blocks from a Burger King and Tile Warehouse.

Opposite the wharf is a sign for the famous Andernach geyser. I go inside and enquire how we can cycle to see this wonder. The woman shakes her head ruefully and explains the only way to visit the geyser is on the ferry moored at the wharf which will take us upstream to a bus and finally to the geyser. It seems as if world's highest cold-water geyser has been claimed by private enterprise. We hop back on our bikes and like Bukowski did early in his life, bid a hasty farewell to Andernach.

We're finally back on the river although the landscape continues to be dominated by small industry. The only cake shop available is attached to a supermarket so we make do with two generic danish pastries and an espresso in a cardboard cup.

Bakeries, cafes, grocers and butchers who serve the local community and are valuable meeting places are slowly being replaced by the single supermarket, impersonal and disinterested. The communities that fight to keep their local services will be the only ones to survive over the coming decades. Under the guise of cheaper prices and one-stop shopping, the supermarket will suck the life and character out of these lovely riverside villages. The sweet taste of the cake only lasts so long.

We're lead into Koblenz by a couple of long-distance cyclists whose tail we latch onto just north of the city. The man on the sturdy road bike is very fast but luckily his wife keeps a slightly reduced pace. We can't get close enough to say hello. Every time I think I'm going to catch them at an intersection, the lights change and he speeds away. Finally, after crossing the Moselle river, I see a sign for Zentrum and turn left. The road-runner couple continue south at the same furious pace.

Koblenz is a meeting place of barge, cruise boats, cable car, ferries, trains, bikes and cars. Or for we wine lovers, where the sweet Moselle meets the steely Rhine Riesling. I love a city ruled in its thousand-year existence by people with interesting names. Louis the Pious. Charles the Bald. Arnold of Isenburg. William the Great.

Cathie the Beautiful and Steven the Hungry park their steeds, Craig the Annoying and Jenny the Reliable under the impressive statue of the Emperor William and gaze across the Rhine at the Fortress Ehrenbreitstein, a pile of stone and artifice atop a cliff, linked to the city by a very alluring cable car. Who'd have thought cable cars swayed so much in the breeze? White-faced tourists ponder whether a walk up a steep hill isn't preferable.

If there's a large hill opposite the confluence of two main rivers, you can bet it has a long history of fortresses. Ehrenbreitstein dates back to the BC era and has been used in numerous *I'm king of the castle* epochs including the Romans, the French, the Prussians, the Nazis and finally to the good citizens of the Rhineland who have converted it into a museum.

This section of the Rhine is known as Deutsches Eck, or German Corner and is dominated by the statue of William the Great who Craig now so slovenly leans upon. Bad bicycle. I move him to a less conspicuous resting place and we gaze up at the former Emperor. He's a handsome chap with a suave moustache and florid hat. While he sits regal and imposing on a horse, a bare-breasted woman stands beside him, holding his crown. William was bombed and dethroned from his stone plinth by the Allies during World War Two. During the partition of the two Germanys, flags of each of the states including those of the East flew at this site in the symbolic hope that one day Germany would be reunited.

Post reunification, after much debate the statue was recommissioned, perhaps less as a symbol of Germany unity then as a nod to history and a lure for tourists. Judging by the crowds today, it's worked a treat. People will travel from far and wide to see a bare-breasted woman.

An avenue of stately plane trees escort us along the Rhine. Young mothers wheel prams, old men lead dogs and we trundle serenely on the orange-leafed carpet, all the way to Konigbacher Brewery. Nice location for a brewery. Pity it's too early for drinking.

The path follows the river and Craig relents from his sullenness to offer me a few more gears. We clackety clack into Rhens, a village overflowing with beautiful houses. At the pub, the handsome owner with long curly black hair regretfully tells us he does not offer lunch, only beer. He suggests we buy a sandwich next door and eat it at his table, washed down with the finest ale. We do. His pub is a storybook pink and white confection with flower boxes, heavy wooden crossbeams and cartoonish drawings of men with hard hats and mermaid tails. No I haven't been drinking too much. The corner house opposite has a magnificent high-pitched slate roof, orange-painted crossbeams and elaborate flower drawings as decoration. All down the cobblestone street are crossbeam houses suitably decorated. We eat under an umbrella pitched in a beer keg and enjoy Koblenzer beer at a pub dating from 1662. Rhens is a marvel.

After lunch we enter the UNESCO Heritage Rhine Gorge, a narrow carving through steep vine-covered hills. At Boppard Corner, a c-shaped bow in the river, the vines grow on a slope that must be close to 40 degrees pitch. I can't believe people can pick grapes on that incline, in soil of brittle shale. And yet, the beauty of Riesling tells me they do. Church steeples dot either bank as we meander along, open-mouthed in wonder.

Boppard is a lovely town of cruise boats, gothic revival villas, numerous white-painted elegant churches and the classicist home of composer Engelbert Humperdinck.

'Why didn't we name one of our children, Engelbert,' I ask Cathie.

'Because it would have been shortened to Bert. Or Bertie.'

'Perhaps Engel?'

'And neither of us can play a musical instrument,' she adds with irrefutable logic.

'Engelbert,' I repeat, rolling the syllables around my tongue.

The villages south of Boppard get prettier and hug the shoreline. Castles and ruins seem to rear above every bend in the river. In this majestic setting, a woman up ahead gets off her tandem bicycle, pulls down her pants and urinates on the path. Her husband discretely looks the other way, while Cathie and I ride past suddenly very interested in the brick wall on the opposite side of the road. When we're safely past and out of earshot, I say, 'She'd been wanting to go for hours and her husband kept promising they'd stop.'

'So to embarrass him, she did it right there,' Cathie adds, 'in front of trucks and cars and ... us.'

'I don't think Craig will ever be the same,' I say.

We enter Saint Goar still a little flushed as it were with *the great pee on the Rhine* incident. Our hotel room has a view of the river and hilltop castle. It also features an armoire for we Seinfeld fans. I neatly unpack my clean lycra and place it carefully in the top drawer. After too many in-jokes about soup nazis and armoire, we retreat to a cafe with a view across the Rhine to the Katz and Maus castles on the far bank. My vote goes to Maus, a brooding medieval two-storey pile with a stern tower. Katz is too modern, too recently renovated for my tastes. We eat dinner at the Restaurant Loreley where a lovely waitress with a bouncing pony-tail serves us Flamekuchen, an uncooked German pizza with cream cheese, onion and ham. It tastes much better than it sounds, especially when washed down with Alt beer. Bless them for importing it from distant Dusseldorf.

In the late evening, I sit at our hotel window watching the lights of the car ferry criss cross the Rhine. Barges rumble down river past the fairytale twinkling of Saint Goarhausen on the far bank.

I do love a fruit salad in the morning, particularly when it's offered alongside scrambled eggs, black bread and a whole jug of coffee served by a man in a burgundy waist-coat who assures us that, 'A car runs on fuel, a cyclist on breakfast.'

The day is noticeably warmer than the past week as we set off eager to see the majestic Lorelei, the rock of legends that has spawned reams of poetry and clashings of heavy-metal rock. We park Craig and Jenny against the riverside wall and stare across at the bare rock soaring 120 metres above the narrowest section of the Rhine. Without wishing to be churlish, the legend heavily outweighs the reality. I love a big rock as much as anybody, but it's the poets and writers who have created the myth. Lorelei in German refers to murmuring water but it's the feminine water spirits of legend that have captivated poets and musicians down the centuries. Heinrich Heine, Apollinaire, Sylvia Plath, Roxy Music, the Pogues all worshipped at the rock of female allure. Artists have a fertile imagination and dare not let reality besmirch a good image. As if to prove its danger, a barge carrying sulphuric acid capsized on this bend as recently as 2011, blocking one of Europe's busiest waterways. One hundred dead poets wailed from their graves, 'I told you so!'

We follow vineyards all the way to Bingen. Even though it's a narrow gorge, there is room for a railway track on either side of the Rhine. The Germans know how to arrange transport. On a small island in the river is the Bingen Mouse tower, a simple white-painted signal tower rebuilt by the Prussians in 1855. The legend of this particular tower involves a callous ruler who steals from his peasants and locks many of them in a barn before setting it on fire. He retreats to his castle only to be chased by a mischief of mice. He flees the mainland to this island, expecting the mice to drown in the river. But the avengers with sharp teeth and scurrying legs survive and corner him in the tower before gleefully eating him alive. I love a legend where the poor gain justice over the rich. If only it happened more in real life. I wonder if Rupert Murdoch is scared of mice? I hope so.

On another island further downstream, the leaves of the trees have all turned orange, even though their brothers on the banks are resisting. The cool temperatures mid-stream have encouraged autumn to arrive early. The clouds loom heavy as we cycle between ploughed fields near the village of Kempten. Two joggers approach as I study my iPad. The short bald man smiles at me and says, 'Bingen that way, Mainz the other.' A few moments later I overtake them and reply in a hopeful voice, 'Mainz it is!'

It begins to rain, so we stop to shrug into our jackets. The joggers catch us and the man can't resist, 'the weather is better in Mainz.' I hope he's correct. At Ingelheim, we retreat to a Sommergarten beside the river. There are two stalls, one selling bratwurst on a roll, the other offering beer. We buy two of each and sit in a large yellow tent watching the ferry cross the river.

'It's the mustard that wins me,' I say, holding up my roll.

'Fat and salt … the perfect accompaniment to beer.' Cathie answers.

The rains eases as Craig clunks along the farmyard paths. We've left the narrow gorge and now cycle through apple orchards and newly-ploughed fields. A woman ahead rides a yellow bicycle with sunflowers tied to her rear rack. The path is lined with small garden allotments, each with a one-room cabin. It's like riding through suburban backyards with lettuce growing in even rows, a shed full of tools and whimsical signs on gates.

Mainz is the capital of Rhineland at the confluence of the Rhine and the Main. It's here we'll turn left and follow the Main all the way to the Czech border. But that's tomorrow. This afternoon, Craig is visiting a doctor. While my elbow has healed, Craig's ailments appear too many to list. I nervously wheel him into a bike shop in the centre of town. The friendly owner puts Craig on a stand and picks and prods him for an inordinately long time.

'You need a new chain, look how loose it is,' he wobbles the chain for effect. 'The sprockets are worn, they are round, so old,' he adds.

Craig shakes on the stand, indignantly.

'If I change chain and sprockets, the bottom bracket must also be replaced. How many kilometres has this bike done?' he asks.

'Over ten thousand,' I tell him.

He shakes his head. 'You will not get to Prague. You also need brake pads and cables for gears. And a new front tyre.'

I wonder if this makeover will give Craig a more friendly and positive personality? I leave him in surgery while Cathie and I check into our hotel. Two hours later, Craig is a changed bicycle, expertly repaired by a young woman who takes him for a quick test ride to check all is well. The cost is substantial but I figure the old fellow deserves it after all these kilometres.

I ride back to the hotel. The gears change in the blink of an eye, the front tyre isn't shaped like an egg, the chain works smoothly. We couldn't be happier. When I take Craig to the garage with Jenny, he eagerly tells her about his makeover. Jenny perhaps wonders what he's done to deserve all the attention while she's been reliable and quiet throughout the whole trip. I hope she understands.

To celebrate Craig's rebirth, we go to church. St Stephen's is on top of the highest hill in town. The Gothic church is highly regarded because it houses nine stained-glass windows created by the artist Marc Chagall. He worked on these elegant masterpieces right up to his death in 1985 at the age of ninety-seven. They are a simple yet ethereal statement on the hope of religion and reconciliation. We wander the interior bathed in a soft blue light and indeed I feel closer to heaven in this beautiful space than any heathen has the right to expect. Chagall's work is carried on by his disciple, Charles Marq who is responsible for the recent addition of nineteen more modest windows.

The church is connected to a historic late-Gothic cloister, a simple garden and surrounding arched thoroughfare which is the resting place of more than six hundred local dignitaries interned over the centuries.

Refreshed in spirit and soul, we eat dinner at the decidedly upmarket Proviant Magazin housed in 19th century ex-military base. Thankfully, the prices don't reflect the surroundings as I tuck into a turkey schnitzel washed down with the local MAB beer served in enamel jugs. I raise my jug, 'To the artists of the soul.'

'And the artists of the bicycle,' Cathie adds.

Let's hope Craig is as renewed as we are.

Chapter Eleven:

Hessen, Germany

Breakfast in a big city hotel amuses me. The quality of food is usually very good. Business people expect lavish offerings and this hotel is no exception - a choice of fresh fruit, juice, yoghurt, eggs any way you please, cheese and ham, all washed down with excellent espresso coffee. It's enough to make a fat businessperson happy which is of course the point. I used to be intimidated walking down to breakfast in lycra and sitting among men and women dressed in expensive suits until I realised two things. Firstly, they were usually too busy scheduling the next meeting on their mobile phone to care who sat next to them. And secondly, they were off to work and I was going on a bike ride. If anything, I should be the smug superior one, not that overweight man beside me in the striped shirt and blue tie and shiny black shoes. He will spend the day trying to sell something. I'll hopefully cruise along a serene river bank, contemplating the ducks and thinking of how much beer I'll drink over lunch as I have none, absolutely zero meetings scheduled for today or tomorrow or any time in the next month. My, these eggs are tasty!

Craig is positively frisky this morning as we cycle across the Theodor Heuss Bridge and along the last five hundred metres of Rhine pathway. It offers a lovely wide vista of the friendly skyline of Mainz. We join a large cruise ship turning onto the Main river. The Main looks timid and genteel as it joins big brother Rhine. The path alternates between bitumen and gravel and we lose sight of the river after only a few kilometres. It's a inauspicious introduction.

Craig purrs along. I realise just how worn out and misfiring he really has been lately. It's nice to have the thoroughbred back. We cycle through vineyards still heavy with grapes. It's very late in the season to be harvesting, but pickers wearing gloves and wide-brimmed hats work row after row in a slow yet time-worn fashion. For the next hour we cycle along the river watching the planes circle in a wide arc waiting to land at Frankfurt Airport. We enter the city on the south bank, passing lines of moored barges now operating as restaurants. We're too early for lunch. It's a case of guessing which bridge to cross to enter the old town.

The one we choose is littered with padlocks attached to every available inch of the structure. On each of the locks are words scrawled in pen.

Jesse and Eva Forever.

Anja and Sam.

Phillip loves Petra.

I hate it. It's nothing more than unoriginal graffiti that defaces public architecture. Started in Paris on the Pont de Arts, this imbecilic fashion is now defacing monuments from the Eiffel Tower to Mount Huang in China. The cynic in me believes the locks will last much longer than the love supposedly expressed by their attachment to a monument. Recently, a railing on the Pont de Arts collapsed under the weight of so many padlocks. The Paris authorities are considering a blanket ban. They should invest in bulk cutters - I'm sure there'd be a long line of we volunteers waiting to remove the locks.

Cathie and I have been together thirty years. We don't need to publicly state our love. Oops, I just did.

The old square in Frankfurt is hosting a wedding, with well-dressed guests streaming out of the rathaus. The crowd is too deep to catch a glimpse of the bride and groom. We retreat to a butcher shop cum restaurant. My bread roll is stuffed with succulent pork and sweet onions, washed down with pilsener. It's absurdly cheap and filling and I'm tempted to order another.

Frankfurt hosts the biggest book festival in the world and while my children's books are occasionally on display at the fair, I have yet to be honoured with an invitation. This year's fair begins next week.

We cycle across another bridge to the Sachsenhausen district and park our bicycles outside an organic gelato cafe on the corner of Bruckenstrasse and Schelstrasse. The waitresses are incredibly friendly and offer excellent cake and coffee which we eat at outdoor tables while watching German hipsters ride fixies down the narrow streets. We should be looking at the tourist sights, but we're content to just hang out in cafes and watch a big city cycle past. It's pleasant to see handsome young people going about their business. We feel more part of the city here than in the Frankfurt Cathedral or taking another photo outside the Opera House. Sachsenhausen in littered with cider bars and cafes and we spend an inordinate amount of time acting like locals.

In the late afternoon, we glide slowly away from Frankfurt along the banks of the Main until we reach Muhlheim and our hotel for the evening. The front door is locked. I knock loudly. No answer. A lady walks past and says, 'This hotel, it's closed.' I look at my watch. She adds, 'No. Closed forever.' She walks across the road and hops into a black BMW. Cathie and I look at each other, not sure what to do next. I lean Craig against the hotel wall and walk around the rear of the building. Three men are rendering the side wall. A man of Turkish appearance climbs down from the scaffold and welcomes me to his hotel.

He shows us the rear garage where we can leave Jenny and Craig and takes Cathie's panniers, leading us upstairs to our room overlooking the street. I ask him if he's busy tonight.

'Eighteen rooms full, two no full,' he says. He offers bottles of mineral water and encourages us to take as many apples from the basket on the counter as we can carry.

I wonder for one unpleasant second whether the lady deliberately tried to steer us away from this hotel. I munch on an apple and try to think of more positive things, like where to eat dinner. Our host recommends just the place.

The restaurant Alte Wagnerei has a huge courtyard of outdoor tables but we choose indoors and are a little embarrassed to be the first diners. Some of the staff are still eating their pre-opening meal. A friendly waitress offers us the menu and a choice of beer and federweisser. We choose one of each. The philosophy of the kitchen is *there is no creative work without tradition*. So how can I not choose a dish translated as *Grandma's Meatloaf*. Cathie orders cheese spatlese. Both meals are wonderful - simple, hearty and yet marvellously tasty. As we're leaving, I notice the line of bike racks in the garden. Cycle friendly as well.

Only twenty-four hours after Craig's makeover, he's causing problems again. Yet another flat tyre. It's no way to start a day. I repair the tube and am perhaps a little rougher than usual in replacing the wheel. I pedal towards the Main river in a funk. It's a cloudy day, chilly with the chance of rain. And an equal chance I'll throw Craig in the slow-flowing Main river and walk to a bicycle shop and buy a new steed.

My mood is lightened considerably on our arrival in Seligenstadt, a delightful town with a Saturday market, street side cafes and enough timber frame houses to start a fire or attract lots of camera-toting tourists. Thankfully, the latter occurs this morning. We snaffle the only available outdoor table at a backerei cafe and order two excellent pastries and coffee. The pedestrian throng is particularly well-dressed as Audis and Mercedes thud over cobblestones in a vain search for parking spaces. The sun is out and all of Germany has decided to visit Seligenstadt.

The Roman Legion set up a barracks on the very spot where we eat our pastry. They held the ground for a paltry one hundred and sixty years before abandoning it. Six hundred years later in 815, a Benedictine monastery was established. Soon after, the remains of the martyrs, Marcellinus and Peter were transferred here to be housed in the newly built Einhard Basilica.

Both buildings remain, although the white-washed baroque monastery no longer houses priests. The Carolingian basilica is a simple red stone church of modest proportions. The real delight is the church gardens. As we stroll the grounds, I count off the vegetables ripe for harvesting. Red and green kale, carrots, artichokes, lettuce, beetroot and spinach - all growing in gardens ringed by apple and pear trees. An old grape vine creeps along the walls, heavy with fruit. Someone tends this place with a devotion often reserved for inside the walls of a church. It's surprisingly quiet, given the crowds in the shopping alleys a few hundred metres away. I guess we all have our place to worship?

My beautiful wife, who has a much keener eye for food than I, sees a sign listing zwiebelkuchen and federweisser outside a cafe down a narrow alley. We order a slice and a glass of each and sit in the sunshine. I wonder how some towns get all the beauty and others have to create their own. Seligenstadt even has its own brewery, established in 1744. The onion tart is so delicious, I order a second.

After lunch, we wander through the numerous streets of timber-frame houses erected in the 17th and 18th centuries. Most have been restored and now house cafes and restaurants or shops selling tourist tat. The price we pay for preserving these lovely old buildings is to open them for commercial purposes.

We eventually leave Seligenstadt and continue down the Main river path, crossing to the north bank soon after Dettingen where in 1743, George the 2nd lead his troops against the French. It was the last time a British monarch would get so close to battle, his ancestors preferring to issue orders from afar or leave the fighting to more experienced commoners. Before the battle began, both sides had agreed to treat any wounded enemy combatants with respect and not regard them as prisoners-of-war, a precursor to the Geneva Convention.

We dawdle into Aschaffenberg, which sits prominently on a hill crowned by the impressive 17th century red sandstone Schloss Johannisburg, a regal tower at each of its four corners. It's an impressive fortress now housing - you guessed it - a museum. Most of the crowds have forsaken the castle for the brewery just across the cobblestone courtyard. It's full to overflowing as waitresses ferry large glasses of amber liquid to overweight tourists tucking into late afternoon schnitzels. We clatter over the cobblestones down to the new town, find nothing as tempting as a brewery with a castle aspect, so head back up the hill to indulge. Aschaffenberg was recently voted number one place to live in Germany in a survey of happy residents. Of course, I've read similar claims for numerous towns all across Europe. But on a sunny afternoon, with the beer flowing, a gentle breeze sweeping up from the river through the orange-leafed oak trees and the flags fluttering on the sandstone turrets, it's hard to argue against such a survey.

Our hotel is across the river in a new town development of empty squares and nondescript houses. The hotel itself is four storeys high and our large room looks back at the castle in the distance. We even have a balcony. I take my wet lycra outside to dry and look across at two old ladies knitting on their balcony. I'm shirtless, but feel I should at least offer a wave. They giggle like schoolgirls in response. The afternoon sags, like muscles on a middle-aged man.

Chapter Twelve:

Bavaria, Germany

As the owners are Italian, I'd hoped for strong espresso this morning. It was not to be, but I hardly notice as I salivate over a perfectly cooked boiled egg. I like them runny. I spoon it out and pile it on a wholemeal bread roll with a few slices of cheese and don't think of coffee again for a few hours.

We cycle alongside the river on a very quiet and misty morning through little villages where rag dolls hang from the front doors of a few houses and immaculate gardens are bordered with wood piles. Occasionally, the mist lifts and I'm treated to aeroplane vapour trails across the blue sky, like the beginnings of a Jackson Pollock masterpiece. At least a few pilots are awake this early. Even the usual dog walkers are safely tucked in their Sunday beds.

Over the past month, I've been tempted by the wild apple trees beside our bike paths. In Australia, these trees would be attacked by hundreds of birds seeking a free feed. Here, they're left in peace. The birds are obviously too gorged on fruit to bother eating every last piece. I pick an apple, taking a tentative bite, expecting it to be soft and unappetising. It's tart, juicy and I take another bite. That's my Sunday morning tea.

Ahead, I spy a luxury cruise ship chugging upstream. I can't resist. A race! I quickly revert to being twelve-years-old again, racing the Scenic Diamond full of people eating a three-course breakfast as I pump away at the pedals. Once I'm in front, I cycle with one hand on my hip, nonchalantly showing who's the fastest. Then I zip ahead while fifty passengers pour another cup of tea and consider how many slices of cheese is too many. In a riverside park, I pull over to take a photo of my sleek defeated rival. Each cabin has double opening glass doors leading to a balcony.

At Worth am Main we stop outside a bakery that is neither a franchise or attached to a supermarket. It's run by a husband and wife team who aren't serving coffee for another hour but their cakes are too good to refuse. I choose a custard slice and eat it outside while watching a few sleepy workers dismantle a temporary stage in the main street. It's seems there was a party last night.

I stifle a yawn. Sundays are for yawning. And eating. And drinking coffee, when we find an open cafe. We wobble down to the river and see our friends in the cruise ship slowly making their way through a lock. The passengers don't look quite so smug as we cycle past, unhindered by river levels and lock masters.

We make it precisely five kilometres to Klingenberg before we're lured into a cafe housed in a railway station. I know what you're thinking - cheap and cheerful with cardboard cups and dispensing machines. Not a chance. This cafe is sleek and spotless with padded leather bench seats and friendly staff. We order our second cake in twenty minutes and an espresso. A gorgeous young couple sit opposite us with their three-year-old son. He sips on a chocolate drink overflowing with cream, managing to get most of it on his cheeks.

Klingenberg was the site of a desperately sad incident in the mid-1970s where a local girl, Anneliese Michel underwent a series of harrowing exorcisms because her parents and two Catholic priests thought she was possessed by demons. It's hard to believe that as recently as forty years ago, a teenage girl with mental illness could be treated in such a manner. Ms Michel died from malnourishment and her parents and the priests were charged with negligent homicide. They were found guilty and received relatively short sentences which provoked an outcry. Two years later, the parents requested their daughter's remains be exhumed and placed in a different coffin. Not surprisingly, the frequency of exorcisms has decreased in Germany since this case. In truth, the number of exorcisms performed anywhere in the first world should be absolutely zero, but the medieval ritual still has supporters within the Catholic Church. Perhaps the mental illness is not only with the patient but also with the institution?

Despite this, Klingenberg is a sunny well-appointed town, slowly waking from its Sunday slumber. And look, there's a familiar cruise ship in the town lock. This time, I can't resist a courteous wave as we cycle away.

To Miltenburg where we learn of a much more positive side to the Catholic clergy. In 2012, the Nazi-aligned National Front were granted permission to march through the village. Father Ulrich Boom was so incensed at this decision that he decided to protest with the loudest weapon in his religious arsenal, the church bells. During the rally, when the first Neo-Nazi began to speak, the appropriately-named Father Boom began ringing the church bells, including the four-thousand kilogram Mother of God bell. The peeling bells drowned out all of the hate speeches and the rally was forced to disband. Father Boom has become something of a folk hero since then. Deservedly so.

Miltenburg is located on a narrow strip of land between the river and surrounding hills. The main street is a picture postcard arrangement of timber-frame houses, a circular fountain in the town square, cobblestones and that lovely church of tolling freedom. I'm pleased to report that Father Boom was recently promoted to Auxiliary Bishop.

The river turns north at Miltenberg and we cycle beside red cliffs and steep vineyards climbing the hills on the left bank. The forest on our side is a few weeks away from autumn glory. There's a muted yellow tone to the leaves. At Freudenberg, the valley widens to meadows of dozing cattle and horses. Sunday cyclists are out in full and who can blame them on such a perfect day. We stop for lunch at a gasthaus near the bridge and eat a tasty sauerbraten. A cruise boat pulls into the wharf, unloading a bunch of passengers dressed in shorts and open-necked shirts. A van stops alongside the ship and two men unload bicycles. The passengers are going to have to work for their lunch.

We cycle absentmindedly for twenty kilometres along the north bank lulled by the green fields, occasional castle ruins on hills and the gentle Main. We pull up at the ferry opposite Mondfeld to take us cross river to our hotel. It's moored on the opposite bank. There appears to be no-one on board. Out of action until ... Monday.

It's such a beautiful day, I'd love to swim across to Mondfeld, but I don't fancy Craig's ability in the water. We cycle a pleasant three kilometres upstream and locate a lock where I carry a fully-loaded Craig and Jenny up and down two flights of stairs to cross the river. Craig smiles smugly and mentions something about me having to carry all the weight, for a change.

The Gasthaus White Rose is located down a suburban street. The owner is a gruff man with a droopy moustache and the personality of a rottweiler. He hands me the room key and points upstairs. I'm too scared to ask if we have wifi. Our room is spartan yet comfortable and looks across the rooftops of the small village.

We eat dinner in the dining room where pictures of the Sydney Harbour bridge hang on the walls. Neither the owner or his wife speak English so we can't ask about the pictures. The beer is cheap, the food acceptable and the owner relaxes a little as the evening progresses. At one point he almost smiles. Although it could have been a grimace.

He certainly smiles the next morning when I pay the bill and tell him, through elaborate mime that he has forgotten to charge me for last night's dinner. Yes, that was a smile. Definitely. He even grunts goodbye. In his defence, he did wake at 7am to serve us breakfast.

Craig and Jenny have slept next to a fridge in the garage and seem none the worse for wear. The mist has returned and almost shrouds the geese flying in arrow formation up river. A dredge works on removing debris from near the lock. I stop to watch. In one huge scoop, it picks up branches, tree trunks and assorted flotsam and swings the load above a large skip on shore. I'm expecting the operator to drop them into the skip from a few metres. I have fantasies of fish falling from the sky. But this man is a meticulous German who carefully lowers his load right into the skip. Diamonds could not have been handled more carefully. I don't see any fish.

Wertheim-am-Main has a castle ruin shrouded in mist and a main street of cobblestones and delivery vans. Most of the shops aren't open yet, except one corner cafe doing brisk business. We cycle past vineyards proliferating in the rich sandstone soil to Homburg where the half-timbered three-storey schloss commands the high ground. I hope no-one is watching as I pick a juicy grape from the vine. At Marktheidenfeld (try saying that after a beer too many), we find a cafe selling real coffee not machine espresso, so it's a machiato and two nutty yet sweet croissants. Make that three.

Because the mist has held so low for the morning, it hardly feels as if the day has begun. We're cruising along the Main next to a dark and typically dense German forest of beech and fir trees. I'm fascinated by the colourful forest floor of mushrooms, fallen leaves and moss-covered logs. A rich earth smell sweeps down the hill, swans glide close to the riverbank and my imagination plays atmospheric mood music to complete the sensory overload. Even Craig is respectfully silent.

At Lohr am Main, another friendly cafe is offering the unbeatable double of zwiebelkuchen and federweisser at the gently persuasive price of Euro 5.50. It's delicious, but I'm so hungry I go further up the main street where a very jovial old lady is sells bratwurst on a roll from a small van. She laughs her way through serving a long line of contented customers.

When we return to the river, I'm once again struck by the number of nut trees growing on public land. For the past fortnight, we've been admiring how many locals scour the ground below the trees for chestnuts. It reminds me of the French villagers we saw picking blackberries last month. In Australia, it's unusual to see such public foraging. We rarely have fruit trees on public land.

There are chestnut trees in the mountains where we live, but no-one collects the newly-fallen bounty. We let them rot on the sidewalk. Some would argue that this is typical of a country at odds with the magnificent natural riches that surround us. While the population have been quick to take up solar panels, living in the hottest continent on earth, our government continues to push the climate-harming industries of gas and coal.

You may think it's a long bow to draw between gathering chestnuts and coal burning power stations. Statistics prove, per head of population, we're one of the largest emitters of greenhouse gas in the world. Shameful evidence of a population and a government not raised to appreciate the seasonal gifts of nature?

At Gemunden, the ice cream shops are doing a brisk business as post-lunch diners relax in the warm afternoon. We haven't booked a hotel for tonight and try our luck at the Tourist Office. The young woman phones the Hotel Atlantis and tells the owner we'll be along shortly. We cycle a kilometre out of town to find the hotel locked and unattended. Back to the Tourist Office and now she suggests a pension up a very steep hill. The ice creams are starting to look very appealing. Our room is underneath the suburban home of a gentle friendly man who speaks no English but knows how to make us feel welcome by offering beer. The clean comfortable room is half the price of Hotel Atlantis which, if you'll pardon the pun, sinks without trace in my memory.

The kindly owner gets up earlier than usual to wait at the front gate for the baker to deliver bread for our breakfast. We bump over the cobblestones of Gemunden and can't find a path beside the river, so battle trucks and early morning traffic for a few kilometres before the misty river announces itself. Back to the path and dodging squirrels who leave it until the last minute before scurrying up a tree.

The morning drifts between open farmland and vineyards on hills. At Zellingen, an old lady wearing a pink cardigan and long white slacks almost falls off her bike as she dismounts near her front gate. She smiles at her clumsiness. Further on, a very old man shuffles along the path with the aid of a walker. He stops every few steps and takes a deep breath. The one constant of this trip is the tenacity of old people walking along our two-thousand kilometre bike path. The countryside in Europe is the province of old people. They work in their gardens, walk slowly to the local shops or sit in parks watching the world pass. Young people migrate to the cities while the old gather nuts and fruit and live as their ancestors have done for the past few centuries, locally and in harmony with the world. As we grow older, the distance of our world shrinks. It's one reason I cycle so much, while my knees hold.

If you can see hillside vineyards, a river, a brooding fortress and numerous cruise boats from the centre of town, then you must be in Wurzburg. As we cycle through the town archway, the clouds grow heavy and threaten rain. It's a postcard pretty town of churches and public buildings stretching from the Baroque to the Gothic with the occasional Renaissance thrown in just to show off. Pity much of it was bombed to ruins in 1945 in a blitz that exceeded the infamous firebombing of Dresden. Ninety percent of the city was destroyed and over five thousand people lost their lives. Undeterred, the citizens, primarily women, set about rebuilding after the war, painstakingly reconstructing the city's notable buildings. It's ironic that women were the saviours of modern Wurzburg, given that over six hundred of their female ancestors were burnt at the stake in the 17th century, condemned as witches by the mad Bishop Philip Adolf. What is it about Adolf as a name for lunatics?

The gently sloping limestone hills near Randersacker are perfect for growing grapes and the town has a number of wine stores and restaurants. The menus are too expensive for our tastes so we continue down the Main. Information boards display photos of the fish we could catch in the river, if we were so inclined. I'm not sure if *nase*, *barbe* and *dobel* are good to eat and given my skills with a fishing line, I doubt I'll ever find out.

At Sommerhausen there's a gasthaus on the river to save us from throwing in a line. We sit in comfortable wicker chairs and drink federweisser and eat Franconia potato soup which tastes more Thai than German. I haven't seen many coconut trees lining the banks of the Main recently. Perhaps the chef is experimenting?

Fortified after lunch, we leave the river path and head up a rather daunting 10% hill to take a shortcut to Sulzfeld. The vineyards watch as we pant heavily past their ripe fruit. This is a very steep hill. I look back and see Cathie and Jenny struggling but refusing to stop. That's my girls! Craig meanwhile has chosen this moment not to offer me the easiest gear, referred to by we cyclists as the *granny gear*. So I grit my teeth and make do with the *elderly aunt gear*.

We're rewarded at the summit with a expansive view past a paddock of deer and horses to the plains below. The only people on this road are farmers on tractors and two girls riding stubborn-looking cart horses who are disinclined to move out of the way to allow exhausted cyclists to pass, despite the prodding of the girls.

On top of the mountain, the road suddenly turns into a forest track of gravel and clay. Oh dear. Luckily we pass two walkers who assure us that Sulzfeld is around here somewhere, but first we should locate Erlach. Up and down and around and yes, just pass that corn field looks like it could be a village.

Erlach, how pleasant it is to cycle down your wide boulevard with not a vehicle to be seen. Look there's a cat asleep on the footpath. A crow watches from the power line. Washing flutters on a second storey balcony. But does anybody live in Erlach? Too late, we're through town and are gathering speed down a very steep hill lined with vineyards.

Sulzfeld reminds me of an Italian village - narrow alleys surrounded by a medieval wall with houses piled seemingly on top of one another as the town rises up a hill. The square has three restaurants and a shady vine-covered array of seats. There are statues of Christ, the holy Mother or arrow-pierced martyrs on each corner house. Green vines creep in and out of gables and over archways, a row of giant angel's trumpets block the doorway to one villa, flower boxes are so overloaded they threaten to topple into the street. And to think it's only one thousand one hundred years old.

Our gasthaus is located down an alley but is closed on Tuesdays. I phone the number listed on the door and a handsome young man with excellent English promises to meet me in five minutes. He leads us to our corner room on the top floor. It has heavy wooden beams on the ceiling, pink and white wallpaper and cute gable windows. We have entered fairyland.

Michael's Kellar restaurant offers the regional dish of half-metre bratwurst with sauerkraut for eight euro. It arrives sizzling on a heated grill, served by the chef and owner's wife. Michael himself makes an appearance later in the evening and asks how far we've cycled. He has wavy grey hair and tortoise-shell glasses and is immaculately dressed in waistcoat and pleated trousers.

'You have seen more of my country than I have,' he says. He offers us another beer.

A farmer drives his tractor into the main square and leaves it idling. He quickly walks to the stone barn we're sitting outside of and opens the wooden doors, before hoping back on the tractor and driving it into the barn. He waves us good evening and enters the yellow-painted house next door with a grape vine curling around the statue of a priest.

There are no other customers at Michael's but it's difficult to leave such a lovely spot. We order two slices of cheesecake instead. The evening unwinds like a vine along a stone wall.

Chapter Thirteen:

Franconia, Germany

I love a town of legends. This morning our first stop is Kitzingen which was founded because the Countess of Schwanberg lost her jewelled scarf which fluttered away from the upper-storey window of her castle. Perhaps she was waving it to her lover? She offered to build a town on the spot where the scarf was found. Sure enough, a peasant named Kitz found it in a sheep paddock beside the Main, where the Countess ordered the building of a cloister.

We cycle through the early morning streets, looking for the leaning tower of Kitzingen. Not content with one legend, this village also offers a much more racy tale concerning workers, wine and Dracula's heart. We eventually locate the tower near a busy intersection. The tower itself is perfectly straight, but the turreted roof has a distinctive lean because the workers used wine instead of water when mixing the mortar to build the peak. The gold ball atop the tower is reputed to hold the heart of Vlad Dracula. The tower leans towards the cemetery opposite where, you guessed it, the grave of Dracula is located. When the sun shines through the tower windows at a certain time of the day, a beam of crosses is thrown across the grave. Poor Drac. His heart is one hundred feet in the sky and cross beams of sunlight torment his rest. Those not involved in the tourist industry in Kitzingen claim the elaborate and rather gloomy grave houses a wealthy old family from the town, but what would they know! I do like the decorative skulls above the grave though. How any of this relates to the Romanian Vlad the Impaler is beyond me, but like the good citizens of Kitzingen I refuse to let facts and logic get in the way of a good story. We leave Vlad and whoever is buried in this lovely cemetery in peace and seek a glorious prize of morning tea.

At Dettelbach, we take a short ferry ride across the river. The captain looks like a cross between the Buddha and a philosopher with a learned beard and serious kind eyes. This serene presence is broken somewhat by the fact that he holds a three-dial gameboy contraption that operates the ferry. The Buddha leads us not to enlightenment but into the thickest mist of the journey. I love mist. I've even written a popular children's poem about the cloying dense stuff. I enjoy the calm it places on the land, like the ever-present hand of a father on a young boy's shoulder. We ride gingerly along a farm road, listening more than looking. The mist coats my beard and leg hair until we have the return of Frosty Man. In the lovely weingut town of Sommerach, a smiling woman with a mop of blond hair and impossibly white teeth serves us our long awaited cake and coffee. A tractor and trailer loaded with wine barrels rumbles through the village as if on cue to prove this is wine-making central.

Downstream there is further proof. Piles of grape skins rot in the weak sun beside wooden barns. Vineyards cover every available patch of ground. In Nordheim, it seems as if every second house is a weingut. It's too early to sample the wine, but I can't resist picking a black grape from the vine. It tastes almost overripe with an excess of juice. Further on the vineyards are wrapped in netting to prevent intrusion, as if the farmers know a thief is on the loose. It's an elaborate process that probably costs more than it saves. Volkach was founded in 906 and hosts a weinfest next week. The air is heavy with a ripe fermented aroma of grapes and mulch.

Five minutes after Cathie says she'd like cheese and wine for lunch, the vineyards disappear. The river opens to fields of corn and grass and there's not a weingut in sight. I suggest we return to Volkach, but we pedal on hoping for the second coming of wine. Alas, the towns are dowdy and spartan, distant cousins to the rich family down the road. We make do with a reheated zwiebelkuchen and drink apple juice in place of wine.

It starts to rain, as if to emphasise we have entered a little-visited part of Germany away from the picture postcards of vineyards and castles and Gothic church spires. The next town is Schweinfurt, an industrial mess of chimneys and bicycle manufacturing. Yes, here's the place to get a proper replacement for Craig. The town was a major ball-bearing manufacturer during the Second World War and was heavily targeted in bombing raids by the Allies. Ball bearings are still produced here, now for the much more benign activity of cycling. I should like Scheinfurt but its devotion to industry makes it somewhat aloof.

We follow the Main in its great loop east, crossing the river at Gadheim. There is very little open in town and there's no sign of our hotel. We ask the locals. They point us to the next village, Ottendorf where our hotel is located up a hill. The owner is an ebullient woman who leads us to our corner room on the top floor. In nearly every hotel we've visited in Germany, our room has been located in the rear corner, often on the top floor. I love it. It means we rarely have a close neighbour snoring through the side wall and occasionally, as in this instance, we get a balcony on which to hang our dripping lycra. I'm not sure if we're allocated this room because we're the first to arrive or because they prefer cyclists located away from business people. In this quiet town, there appears to be no other guests at all.

This is confirmed at dinner where we dine alone. It gives us time to chat to the owner who tells us of their holiday plans at Christmas beside the North Sea.

'Isn't it cold?' I ask.

'Ja. Freezing,' she smiles, 'but the air is clean and my family and I walk. We walk for two weeks. Doing nothing but breathing.' She takes a deep breath and smiles at the thought.

'Like on a bicycle,' I say. 'Nothing to do but pedal and breathe,' I cut into my pork steak, 'and eat!'

The meal is a strange concoction of home made ingredients. Pork with mushrooms, onions and ... grapes! And a side of walnut bread. Cathie has rosti with cheese and tomato. It seems as if our host has used whatever she had in the kitchen. It's delicious all the more because it's so evidently home made. After dinner, we wander up the hill to the vacant fields. A full moon rises over the river and to our left the local football team trains - their voices rise to meet us. When we return to the hotel, our host is sitting in the courtyard shelling walnuts, for her next loaf of delicious bread.

In the morning, we meet her husband who is even friendlier, if that's possible. Waking at 6:30 to make breakfast doesn't wipe the smile from his face. With limited English, he makes a joke of my credit card when I offer it for payment. It has a see-through section near the microchip. He says the card is invisible and so is the money. At least I think that's what he means. He helps us remove Craig and Jenny from their den and wishes us a good journey, waving from the double gate.

Hassfurt is a delightful village of cobblestones and immaculately preserved wooden-frame houses. It also has three cafes open very early this morning, but it's hard to justify cake after only four kilometres of cycling. We continue to Augsburg where the combination of thick mist and a lack of signs leads us astray. Barking dogs, dead-end campgrounds and endless corn fields. After thirty minutes of wandering, we give up and return to Augsburg and follow the main road to Zeil. It's not as pretty as Hassfurt but it does have a chirpy young woman in a backerei who shows us four tea cakes - rhubarb, cherry, apple and berry. We choose rhubarb and berry.

Can a day turn on something as sweet and simple as a tea cake? Zeil has little charm but my mood improves dramatically. We're back beside the river and although the mist continues to cloak each village in a damp fug, I happily commit to the task at hand. Limbach and Eltmann have no shops but each has a brewery. The Limbach brewery has two giant brass-coloured tanks. I wonder if the beer is a similar rich colour? Through Dippach, Rosstadt, Trunstadt, the mist reveals only the neon lights of each shopfront and the locals wrapped in jackets and scarves.

We arrive in Bamberg and the mist magically lifts as if embarrassed to hide the riches of this beautiful town. We plunge into the UNESCO World Heritage listed old town, cycling along the area known as Little Venice. Any town with houses close to the water wears this unfortunate moniker, but Bamberg does not suffer from the comparison. The hoard of camera-wielding Japanese tourists forces us to dismount and walk through the streets.

Modern tourists remind me of big-game hunters in Africa - we point and shoot with our digital cameras, reload and shoot again, and rarely take the time to look at the magnificent object we're capturing. When I find myself doing this, I put away the camera and take notes instead. This helps my memory and encourages me to see more than just a two-dimensional object.

I stand on the old bridge and consider how many humans have contributed to building this majestic town in the past one thousand years. A white water kayak course is set up on the rapids next to the 14th century rathaus. Not that the competitors would get much chance to enjoy the view. We wander uphill to the Bamberg Cathedral with its four towers and statue of the Bamberg Horseman, a symbol of the town. He looks decidedly regal and his name is Stephen, so I like him very much. The interior of the church wavers between the Gothic and Romanesque with the added flourish of a Pope's tomb. The 11th century Pope Clement 2nd reigned for just twelve months and is the only Pontiff buried outside of Italy and France. The founder of the Cathedral, Emperor Henry 2nd is buried in a magnificent marble tomb, with carvings of his wife and himself in repose on the lid. Which proves if you want a nice location for your eternal rest, it's wise to build a cathedral.

A shaggy beggar on the stairs leading down to the old town asks for money so I relieve my jersey of its coins. Craig and Jenny are where we left them opposite a very busy restaurant. The waiters have a nice patter so we decide to give it a go. I don't need a menu. Instead I point at the meal the gentleman three tables away is eating.

'Scherfela. Pork shoulder,' the waitress says.

'And beer,' I smile.

'Of course,' she answers.

Cathie chooses pork belly. Both meals are delicious. My scherfela has crisp crackling and juicy meat and comes with a sweetly sour kraut. Or a sour sweet kraut?

A local sits down beside us on the long table and says hello. The waitress brings him a beer. His meal arrives soon after, as if the kitchen has been waiting for his arrival. I'm impressed. The waitress and he begin a long friendly conversation. We tourists can wait, as it should be. He reads the paper during his meal of sausages and sauerkraut, only looking up when it's time to depart. He leaves a tip and wishes us a good day, tucking the paper under his arm before strolling back to work. A contented man.

On the way out of town, we pass three bike shops on the same street interspersed between backereis and sex shops. Everything is closed for lunch, even the red light shops. We trundle along the river to our hotel in the village of Kemmern. The hotel is rather modern and situated near the main road. The receptionist gives us our key and tells us we're on the top floor. You guessed it, a corner room with lovely full length windows opening out to a Juliet balcony. Craig and Jenny don't fare quite so well, relegated to under an umbrella in the rear garden. Craig mutters something as we walk away. I'm sure I'll regret it tomorrow.

The Wagner Brauerei has been trading since 1788 - the year white Australia was founded. The Wagner is overflowing with locals who have all cycled here, judging by the number of Craig's brothers and sisters crowding the parking space. Everyone is drinking from half-litre jugs and waiting for the kitchen to open in an hour. The barman brings Cathie a pilsener and me a 'brown' beer, which to my innocent eye should be labelled a *burnished gold* beer.

After the obligatory schnitzel and chips, we order another beer and admire how many full glasses the waitress can carry. I'm impressed by how Germans pour their beers. They aren't afraid of froth and will happily keep topping up the glass until there's a few centimetres of genuine *head* on the brew. In Australia, bar workers spend an inordinate amount of time tilting glasses at just the right angle to control the froth.

Too often it's not enough, but they serve it anyway. The consistency of beer in Germany shames we southern upstarts. When we go to the bar to pay, the owner offers us a taste of his smoked beer. I hate smoked beer, but this one is subtle and refreshing not heavy and sour. It's kept in wooden barrels and the smoking process is a secret.

This brewery has been part of the community for over two hundred years providing employment, identity and social cohesion. I can't think of a better place to spend Thursday night under a full moon.

Last night, I consulted the great god Google and plotted a number of haphazard alternate routes across and over the hills of Upper Franconia rather than slavishly following the ever-dwindling Main river. I fancied the idea of being on top of a hill gazing at uninterrupted farmland rather than the narrow valleys we've been following since entering Germany.

My dream lasts thirty minutes in the mist this morning. We start on the wrong road - someone yells 'autobahn' from a passing vehicle to warn us where we are heading. We execute a quick u-turn and try two other nondescript backroads. I yearn for the simplicity and thoughtlessness of satellite navigation.

After an hour of misty dead-ends, we give up and return to the ever reliable Main. In each of the following three towns, I scout for alternate routes up and over the hills, but if the German Radweg system suggests you keep to the waterways ... well then that's what you do.

The towns seem unusually quiet today. We reel off the kilometres, alternating between cycle paths along the river and through rolling farmlands. The sun streaks through the mist as we eat cheesecake and contemplate how far we have to cycle today. I'd been hoping to avoid the crooked wanderings of the river when I booked a B&B in Bad Berneck, a town in the Fichtelgebirge mountains near the Czech border. Now we are Main-bound, the distance has blown out to over one hundred kilometres. There's nothing to do but plough ahead.

At Bad Staffelstein, the imposing 18th century Basilica of the Fourteen Holy Helpers is under scaffold while the band of fifty-six holy workers attempt to restore it to former glory. The interior is a white confection of murals and an altar that represents the aforementioned holy saints. The fourteen healers include Giles who represents a good confession; Vitus who helps epilepsy, and the virgin martyr Margaret of Antioch who represents childbirth. One could say miraculous indeed.

We finally reach Burgkunstadt in the early afternoon and cycle up a hill to the town square where all the restaurants are closed except a small cafe with a verandah overlooking a handsome yellow and white-painted church. The cafe is overrun with customers on this sunny day. We both order chilli con carne. One dish arrives in ten minutes, another thirty minutes later. We lean back, look at our watch and wonder how long we'll be cycling this evening. I study the iPad map and calculate alternate routes. It seems we're heading for Kulmbach, after lunch.

And what a lovely town it is. An oompha poompha band plays in the park, the beer flows readily and everyone we ask for directions to Bad Berneck shrugs in a very friendly but ultimately unhelpful way. We retreat to a gelato bar and contemplate the map once more. It's a pity we can't spend too long in Kulmbach as I later learn that the castle on the hill houses the largest toy soldier collection in the world. It's also where the Main river, our friend for the past five hundred kilometres splits into two tributaries - the red and white Main. The white Main is a fresh little stream with overhanging autumn trees. We follow the river alternating between a lovely path and a back road through a narrow valley.

At Ludwigschorgast, we must choose between the left and right fork in the path. We have no idea which way to go. Although my politics always lean left, this time I choose right. Within a few hundred metres, the road pitches up steeply. We climb for thirty minutes and are treated to a wonderful view of rolling green fields and distant mountains. Those hills are our destination tomorrow. We stay on the plateau for only a few kilometres before dropping down into the valley. We should have chosen the left fork which meandered along level ground. That'll teach me. Always left!

A busy highway appears to be the only route to Bad Berneck. And then our angel of the mountains arrives. Dressed in corduroy jeans and a fleece jacket, the bearded gentleman on a mountain bike asks where we're heading. He lives in Bad Berneck and knows a shortcut. After one hundred and ten kilometres, *shortcut* is the word I most want to hear. We cycle through lovely back lanes, past cow paddocks and gentle grassy hillsides talking about football and the German national holiday which is ... today. To commemorate the reunification in 1990, all of Germany now celebrates on October 3rd, when the formal agreement was signed. Many people wanted alternate dates, but eventually it was decided a holiday is a holiday and a united Germany deserves one that recognises that joyful event. Who am I to quibble. I'm being lead to the door of my B&B by a friendly German man who would otherwise be at work on this Friday afternoon. Thank you Gunther!

Our B&B is rather strange, a combination of an Eastern European guesthouse, cafe and private home. The owner and her son are very friendly. Craig and Jenny are offered a dusty barn crammed with tractors and building materials and we're treated to a simple three-course home-cooked meal of cabbage soup, followed by cabbage rolls stuffed with mince and stewed apples for dessert. The beer is cheap, our room is spacious and a stream trickles past our window.

It's our last night in Germany. Too readily Germans are regarded as abrupt and rather taciturn. Some would say severe. Perhaps their language tends to make them sound that way? The dialect has none of the romance of French or Italian. But we've found the people to be unfailingly polite and friendly, eager to please and possessing a subtle and sometimes dark humour. And best of all, they know how to design bike paths. Without a map, we've been able to negotiate our way across the country with a minimum of fuss. Yes, we had to keep to the prescribed path today, but that's hardly the fault of the German cycleway system. We're already contemplating our next visit. Talk is of cycling from Berlin to Copenhagen. But don't tell Craig.

Chapter Fourteen:

Fichtelgebirge Mountains, Germany

A gently rising path scattered with newly-fallen leaves, the gurgling White Main and the early morning sun filtering through the birch forest. Fifteen kilometres of perfection. It's eight degrees and high clouds float above the hills, but we're safely enveloped by this forest path away from the whine of trucks labouring up the mountain. With a steady gradient of 4%, we climb three hundred metres in an hour before arriving at Biscofgrun, a tiny alpine ski village. It's too early in the season for anything to be open except the service station.

We cycle up a very steep road where the Euro Velo 4 map suggests a forest path. Pity it's not signposted. There are numerous logging tracks. Each new path looks darker and gloomier than the last. I suck in a deep breath and choose the next one. It pitches us into heavy cloud and we shrug into waterproof jackets and gloves. I come across a logging truck but the windows are covered in curtains, the driver asleep. Lucky for some. The track is eroded into corrugations. The left fork goes downhill, the right fork uphill. We share a Snickers while choosing. I check my watch. We've been wandering these forest paths for an hour and I have no idea where we are. It feels as though the border is just ahead, up the steep right fork.

Four men arrive at the crossroads on well-worn mountain bikes. I'm not sure which of us is more surprised to find others out on this lonely mountain. They speak a little English. I ask directions to Roslau, certain they'll recommend the right fork, the way my limited map implies. The youngest rider says, 'Left.'

'No, that's the way to Vondorf,' I say.

He smiles and points to his oldest companion, 'He will know. IT expert!'

I take my iPad over to this chap and he looks at it rather dismissively before showing me a detailed map on his smartphone. A purple dot shows our current location. He traces his finger along the left fork leading all the way to Roslau. I'm so happy I could hug him.

'Where did you begin,' the youngest rider asks.

'St Malo in France,' I answer.

They all seem impressed, except the IT expert.

'All that way, to be lost in the German forest,' he grins.

We all laugh.

We shake hands and they pedal briskly up the right fork. We breeze downhill, the sun brightens, a well pours a steady stream of mountain water from an ancient tap and the trees offer a welcoming archway as we enter the village of Meierhof. We come to another crossroads. Again, I think it's right. I ask a farmer. Again, I'm proven wrong. When will I ever learn?

There are no restaurants in Roslau, so we make do with a delicious custard cake and coffee from a backerei. We check our limited online map again.

'Let's ignore it and keep to the roads,' I suggest.

Cathie raises an eyebrow. She doesn't have to say anything.

'The roads are quiet,' I say. 'And I'd rather be lost on bitumen than in a forest.'

She offers me the last slice of cake, in agreement.

It's an up and down morning, alongside recently ploughed fields on the plateau and clumps of forest on the hills. Wind turbines dance above us and I suddenly realise that we're within a few hours of cycling into our fifth and final country of this trip. We've ridden two thousand three hundred kilometres and in Germany followed two lovely river valleys on the Rhine and the Main. But here on the high plateau we have rich grasslands, dark German forest and a chorus of birds to farewell us.

My mood gets even better when the road tilts noticeably downhill and we glide all the way to Thiersheim which is advertising the possibility of a whopping forty thousand Euro grant to buy property in town. I stare at the sign. That's a rather large giveaway for such a small town. In small print is a warning alerting the current residents that the 'sour wells in Kothigenbiberbach' have contaminated the town drinking water and it should be boiled before consumption. Oh dear. It's still a lovely town. Just don't drink the water.

In Schirnding, we finally reunite with a bike path that takes us beside a lovely stream where a stone plinth is inscribed with a quote from Gandhi and an obelisk displays the names of Jewish people who live in the region. Neither appear to be related to the war. A few hundred metres further on, we come across an orange bike sign, listing only towns in the Czech Republic. On the opposite side are German towns. We have reached the border. We celebrate with a Snickers bar and water.

'How many words do you know in Czech?' I ask.

Cathie bends her thumb and forefinger into a large zero.

'Me too,' I say.

'It looks like the chicken dance for lunch,' she laughs.

Once in Bulgaria, in a very small town where no-one spoke English, I ordered chicken at a restaurant by putting my hands under my armpits and flapping in a rather poor imitation of a rooster. They served us chicken.

Every time I cross a border, I try to spot the differences. I'm sure some are just imaginary because my senses are heightened by the thrill of entering a new country. Here, my first two responses are the land is less cultivated and there are more birds. Off to our right is a mess of buildings that were the Customs checkpoint in the Soviet era. We're in that curious wasteland between countries, a patch of ground that nobody seems to claim as their own. Except perhaps the birds.

The first Czech building is a modern glass Casino. I'm a little surprised.

'Hey, I'll get some Czech money from the ATM,' I say to Cathie.

'Nice gambling attire,' she says, looking at my lycra.

'Nowhere to put my winnings,' I grin.

I become the first man to enter a casino in lycra, perhaps apart from Liberace in his heyday. My stay is short. A beautiful young woman in an orange uniform shakes her head when I make elaborate ATM gestures. She points east and says, 'In town,' in very good English. I think she means Cleb, which is ten kilometres away. Except, we've booked a hotel just down the road.

We have entered the land of the unpronounceable. Pomezí nad Ohrí is a village near the Skalka Dam on the river Ohre. The florid accents above certain vowels indicate an 'oo' instead of an 'ah' or an 'ug' instead of a 'doh'. Something like that. Pomezí began as a farming village in the 13th century, degenerated into a slate quarry in the 16th century and remains a lonely outpost, albeit one with a casino, in modern times.

The hotel is a simple two-storey stone building with six shuttered windows above and a long terrace where drinkers can look at the expanse of Lake Skalka. I enter through the front door and am greeted by a beautiful waitress. Are all Czech women beautiful? I tell her I have a booking. She looks concerned.

'It is no more,' she says.

'Tonight,' I say, perhaps unnecessarily. 'Booking dot com.'

'Yes,' she nods, 'We are full.'

'But I have a booking,' I repeat.

I fear we are getting nowhere. I take out my phone and show her the booking.

She sighs.

'You had booking. But we cancel, because full,' she says.

She may be beautiful, but at the moment she is not very nice.

She attempts a smile. 'Please, one moment.' She rushes into the kitchen. I hear voices through the swinging door. Her voice appears to be winning the argument. She returns, a slight flush to her perfect cheeks.

'I'm very sorry. We cancel. Company not tell you.'

I'm beginning to understand. I ask if I can use their wifi to go online. She reads me the password. In my mailbox is an email from the website confirming the hotel is overbooked and my booking is cancelled.

'Very sorry,' she repeats.

Now it's my turn to sigh.

She touches my wrist and says, 'But, you wait and I fix.'

It's well past lunch time. I ask if we can eat here.

She smiles. At last, there is something she can offer us.

We take a seat at the front bar and order chicken without having to flap my arms. And two excellent Czech beers. The food is hearty and impossibly cheap. The beer costs less than a dollar Australian. If only we could stay here.

The waitress, who I later learn is the owner, returns and tells me they will make room for us, but can we wait an hour, please. We sure can. I order more beer. True to her word, she returns in an hour and leads us upstairs to a large room with bright green and yellow walls and a wonderful view over the lake. The toilet is across the hall, but the room itself is splendid. I bow before her beauty and generosity.

Before dinner we walk up the hill overlooking the village. On a Saturday in the fading light, workers are excavating a large construction project which I suspect is a highway bypassing the village. Or perhaps it's just a very impressive bicycle path linking the two countries?

It's a lovely view up here, the lake stretching east framed by wooden mountains on the horizon and neat fields in the foreground, the village defined like so many, by the church steeple and main road.

The owner suggests I try the Czech national dish of Svickova - beef sirloin with bread dumplings, cranberry and cream sauce. It's heavy comfort food for long rural winters. I also learn that the Czech Republic pips Australia for having the highest beer consumption per capita in the world. I can't blame them. The quality of the beer is sensational. I sleep like a drunk baby.

Chapter Fifteen:

Karlovy Vary, Czech Republic

Sophia, the owner of this hotel, should set up a franchise at every entry point into the Czech Republic because she is the epitome of welcome. She wakes at dawn to serve us a delicious breakfast of eggs, ham and cheese. We saw no other guests during the evening. I wonder how many rooms this place has? Perhaps she'd decided to give herself a Saturday night away from guests until we turned up and she just couldn't say no?

The weather is cool and hazy as we cycle along the quiet Sunday into Cheb. Entry into town is on a leafy path through a thick birch forest on the lake. A single gravestone tilts at an odd angle towards the path. I wonder where the other graves are located? Are we riding over them? On the far side of the lake a yellow double-storey house sits aloof on the water's edge, gazing back at the walled town. The path wanders down to the shore and then skirts past a block of ugly six-storey apartments.

Over the years we've travelled regularly in Eastern Europe and I have a list of certain images that define the region for me. Number One is crumbling apartment blocks. In the communist era, small-scale farmers were banished from the land in favour of State-run enterprises. The displaced families were housed in these decaying apartments and sadly many rural communities were lost. This apartment block in Cheb has at least been repainted and looks like it may stand for another decade or two before toppling into the water.

My second Eastern European image walks ahead of us on the path - an old lady wearing a coloured headscarf and a shapeless black dress. Sometimes these women appear as wide as they are tall. They look at the world with a stern unflinching glare as if they have witnessed too much.

Cheb began as a Slavic stronghold in the 9th century. Over the years it's been invaded by various tribes and because of its proximity to the border has been prized by imperial armies. The Swedes, Austrians, Germans and Slavs have all laid claim. Hitler regarded the Sudetenland as German and it was the first target of his army marching eastward. Cheb became a German enclave. At the end of World War Two, the region was returned to Czechoslovakia and the German population were expelled west.

It has a splendid main square, on this Sunday morning invaded by two peaceful Australians. We lay claim to the long cobblestone expanse in the centre and regard the magnificent surrounds of elegantly painted houses as just reward for our many kilometres. It looks suitably wealthy here in town away from the outlying crumbling apartment blocks.

We follow a back road beside a gorgeous stream that doesn't have banks, it appears to float through the landscape. I wonder what happens when it floods? Or perhaps it's in flood now which explains the absence of a bank?

At Chvojecná, a football game is in full swing. Two teenage girls watch as a bunch of young men battle. Up ahead a covered bridge crosses the river. It's a dark timber masterpiece that deserves to be traversed by a horse and buggy not two clanking bicycles. We stop mid-stream and look down at the clear water. I wonder if the teenage girls and their boyfriends hang out here, after the game. It's impossibly romantic. I reach for Cathie's hand.

'What's up,' she says.

'It's beautiful,' I respond.

She rolls her eyes. 'You want to go back and watch the football game, don't you?'

'Only for a few minutes,' I say.

Refreshed with love and football, we cycle back over the bridge and onwards to Eastern European Image Number Three - the massive railway station in the middle of nowhere. Winner of this prize is Dasnice. In a clump of woods sits a large yellow decrepit building of stone and steel. Six train lines run past a crumbling concrete platform. Six lines! Why so much infrastructure? I assume it was for Soviet troop movements. It's certainly not for passengers visiting this village. The station building has numerous office windows on the second floor. I imagine people live up there now. The lower vestibule is open but there's no-one around and no sign of train timetables or a functioning ticket window. I love the place, despite its bleak future.

We cycle up a heavily forested path and come upon a block of flats that look derelict, except for a family of gypsies in the front yard. From under a tree, a man yells at his two companions hammering at the wheel of an overturned car. I don't fancy their chances of removing the wheel in that fashion. The roadside is scattered with rubbish. We turn a corner and a huge pile of car tyres clutter the hill. In the valley ahead is a power station. I assure Cathie we won't be heading that way. At the next crossroads, we descend straight towards the beast of a power station.

Steam billows from its two large chimneys, but also escapes from numerous smaller funnels and pipes and gaping holes, thereby fulfilling Eastern European Image Number Four - large infrastructure projects that continue to serve long past their use-by date. It's as if the whole thing could explode at any minute. It's the noisiest power station I've ever heard - a big belching monster painted an innocent shade of apricot.

The workers for this beast live in the nearby town of Sokolov, which festers along the Ohre river, a clump of eight-storey apartment blocks showing desperate signs of concrete cancer. We keep to the river path. On the opposite bank is a one-metre diameter pipeline. I'm struck by its age and how it's housed in a rusting metal frame that prevents anyone from climbing under or over it to get to the river. I'm sure it's still in operation or else the citizens of Sokolov would have taken to it with a blowtorch to access the water.

For the past few hours we've been following a well-signposted cycle route through villages of grinding poverty where people are dressed in very old clothes, the buildings are decrepit and the few shops are closed or out of business. And yet, the signposts look fresh and new. We haven't seen fellow long-distance travellers and will be surprised if any appear. It's a little confusing.

Some countries deserve their own colour. Whenever I think of Australia, I see the colour brown - in the dirt of the outback, the suntanned skin of its inhabitants and the burnt dry grass of my suburban backyard.

My nominated colour for the Czech Republic is yellow. All day we've cycled past villages where the majority of houses are painted lemon, the churches are yellow or apricot and the forest paths are lined with gold-leafed trees. In spring, the rape fields are radiant gold. In these towns of hopeless poverty, maybe yellow eases the gloom?

We continue beside the river for ten kilometres to the ancient town of Loket. The stone castle with yellow turrets towers above the river. A goat herd springs lively on its steep slopes. The path to the town square is up a cobblestone lane of 18% gradient. Loket means 'elbow' in English - the town is framed by the river on three sides, in the shape of a bent elbow. The castle dates from the 15th century while parts of the central square are 16th century including the baroque city hall. It's a lovely spot for lunch and we choose a restaurant with outdoor tables, despite the chill.

After thirty five days and perhaps one hundred meals on this trip, we experience our first poor lunch. The house special of roast deer with spinach and mushroom dumplings is not special at all. Fat grisly meat and dry hard dumplings does not make a good combination. We leave most on our plates and walk across the square to where a young man is cooking chimney cakes over a charcoal grill. I love chimney cakes - cylindrical donuts in the shape of a chimney - covered in cinnamon and sugar. The statue on the fountain is of Jesus with gold arrows through his chest. Rumour has it he preferred this exquisite torture to the taste of old deer from the town restaurant. As I'm admiring his sacrifice, eight teenage girls walk past singing 'ba ba bah ba ba bah' in loud harmony.

So begins a romantic afternoon of golden forests, a fast-flowing river and cute wooden bridges near rocky bluffs. On one suspension bridge, we stop mid-stream and watch two young men climb a vertical cliff, fifty metres above disaster, held secure by a rope and hook. From a restaurant opposite, people drink beer and take photos of the intrepid pair.

We follow the signs into Karlovy Vary. A posse of ice-hockey fans, wearing the team jersey and scarves chant along the bike path and we reluctantly choose the main road and an express entry into the old town.

Wow! What a town. Home to thirteen hot springs and a bewildering number of ornate Art Nouveau buildings, it's a confection of pastel stone and ornamental iron, nestled in a narrow valley at the confluence of the Ohre and Tepla rivers. We cannot believe the number of beautiful buildings. Boulevard after boulevard of Art Nouveau splendour - curved stone mouldings above windows and on balconies, organic whiplash decorations on iron railings, angel heads, flowing robes - it's like walking through an oversized art gallery.

In the old town, the ornate spa baths have extended verandahs and colonnades where fountains pour steaming spring water out of taps frosted white with mineral salts. People line up to fill china mugs. Everyone wanders the streets sipping from these mugs, which can be bought from souvenir shops at vastly inflated prices. I can't resist. I empty my water bottle and hold it under the stream for a few seconds before taking a sip. It's scolding hot and tastes excessively salty and sour. I tip it out. I'll get my *health benefit* from a sour bicycle named Craig rather than a mineral spring, thanks.

The Heluan Hotel is located up a hill behind the colonnade spa. The friendly receptionist gives us a front room on the fourth floor overlooking the old town. I feel like royalty. Our room has high ceilings, big windows and a two metre tall heater from the Victorian era. We wash away the grit of seventy kilometres and dress in every article of warm clothing we have. It's getting cold during the evenings and we haven't packed enough.

We wander down to the Tepla river at the foot of our street. Steam rises from the surface. Ducks bask in the warm water. Dumped unceremoniously over the river is the Soviet-era spa building that looks hopelessly out of place amongst all this Art Nouveau majesty. Like a toad at a butterfly exhibition, it spits in the face of capitalist wealth and privilege. I wonder why the government doesn't just pull it down. Rebuild. Or leave the river to flow untouched through the old town.

The French architect Le Corbusier described Karlovy Vary as a 'rally of cakes' alluding to the pastel coloured buildings with decorative flourishes of stone and plaster. It's hard not to walk around without looking up at each building to see what majesty sprouts from above. Oops, just tripped over the cobblestones. Pardon me.

I'm tempted to stay another day in Karlovy Vary. We spend an enjoyable evening after dinner researching the 'health treatments' we can get tomorrow. For one hundred euros, we can enjoy *gum irrigation, instrumental lymphodrainage, a hotstone massage* or my favourite, *oxygen inhalation*. It also costs a small fortune to swim in the warm salty mineral baths.

'Isn't it pleasing there are people rich enough to breathe oxygen,' Cathie says, sarcastically.

'Stupid enough, you mean,' I add.

'Isn't *gum irrigation* just cleaning your teeth?' she asks.

'Probably, but it is with the magic water,' I grin.

We return to our hotel room where I indulge in self-administered gum irrigation before spending a recuperative night of oxygen replenishment and horizontal deep-sleep aromatherapy - that is, I sprayed some deodorant in the room before falling asleep.

The real reason we decide to spend another day in Karlovy Vary, apart from the splendid architecture is the Freedom Cafe. When you stumble across the best coffee in Eastern Europe, it's wise to visit a few times. Down a side street in the upper town, it's a warm haven of friendly staff who serve excellent buckwheat pancakes with honey and banana for breakfast, wonderful bruschetta and salads for lunch and a baked carrot cake for afternoon tea. Yes, we return three times during the day. Pity they're not open for dinner. It's all home made of course and unlike much of Eastern Europe, they know how to use olive oil. The two women owners tell us about their holiday in Greece as they ply us with coffee.

'We've eaten a lot of food during the past forty days, but today I feel nourished,' Cathie says.

'And much cheaper than a colonic irrigation,' I offer.

Apart from lounging around a coffee shop, we ride the funicular up the hill to the Diana Tower, built in 1914 and offering a splendid view of the wedding cake town below. After all the food we've eaten, it's fun to climb the one hundred and fifty steps to the watchtower and gaze across the autumn mountains.

'We have a long climb out tomorrow,' I say.

'I need another carrot cake,' Cathie replies.

Come on, it's our rest day.

Chapter Sixteen:

cycling to Bohemia, Czech Republic

We're the first guests at the hotel breakfast this morning and have a vast array of cakes and croissants and cheese and other indulgences to choose from. Other couples begin arriving soon after and pile cakes on their plates like they've entered an eat-all-you-can-before-the-concierge-kicks-you-out-competition.

Refreshed after a rest day, I retrieve Craig from the boiler room only to discover he has a flat tyre. Yet again. So much for the early start. As punishment, I make him climb a very unsavoury set of cobblestones. It's so steep, I have to hop off and push. I ask Craig if he plans to be a good boy today. He doesn't answer or I can't hear him over my puffing. Once free of cobblestones, we climb a winding backroad snaking through the forest towards the airport. It's a rare airport that's situated on a mountain, so I expect we'll descend soon. No such luck. We keep climbing and eventually are thrown onto the main highway to Prague. Oh dear.

It's not pleasant, but given the conflicting Google map options, is the only sensible choice. A truck thunders past my left ear and I wonder if *sensible* is the correct word. We pedal uphill into a dangerous mist. I wish Craig and Jenny had lights. The mist gets thicker, the road shoulder thinner and we blunder along for ten scary kilometres before finding an alternative. If yesterday was a rest day, today is a stress day.

The only shop open at Bochov is a service station which offers apple strudel and coffee. The mist doesn't look like lifting anytime soon and the hoped for alternative proves to be a dead-end so it's back to the highway for another frightful five kilometres before we turn off onto a bumpy road to the village of Urdc. It's not really a village, just a few downbeat houses and a threadbare five-storey apartment block of flaking paint and timber bolted where window panes should be.

'We're twenty minutes drive from sheer opulence and indulgence ... and look at this.' Cathie says.

The thought had crossed my mind. This is grinding poverty made all the more bleak by the harshness of the weather and yet Karlovy Vary is built upon the whims of the wealthy who pay a small fortune to have entirely worthless things done to their bodies in the name of good health and beauty while these people scratch around for a living.

It's as if the village names hint at the poverty within - Urdc, Polom, Ratibor. To get to Ratibor we follow a bike path that descends steeply into a dark forest. The path is worn away by erosion, so much so that Cathie has to frequently hop off and push. Craig and I clunk over one bump after another. It's not so much a path, more a mountain bike obstacle course. If this is the Euro Velo 4, then it needs some serious work. In Ratibor, which consists of four houses, a barn and green slime-covered pond, I check Google maps and decide to plot my own route away from the EV4.

We keep to the roads, such as they are. The route winds through a birch forest until we reach Zlutice, which on Google looks like a big town. No. It's bleak and lonesome.

The road sign to Chyse points left but someone has taped across the name of the town as if to say the road is blocked. Indeed, just ahead is a bollard in the middle of the bitumen. We nervously ride around it to find two workers dozing in a car. I ask if this is the way to Chyse? They shrug, but seem to indicate we can continue. We pass a vacant tractor parked in the middle of the road and the surface improves dramatically. It's the best we've seen in the Czech Republic. A stream appears on our right and leads us all the way to Chyse. When roadwork occurs in rural areas, they close the whole road rather than putting in counter-flows. Ideal for cyclists.

Chyse has a lovely white-painted church, brightly coloured apartment blocks in a good state of repair and Eastern European Image Number Five - the grocery store in someone's front room. I'm never sure if these places are co-ops only for residents of the village or just an enterprising soul who has crowded his front room with cereal packets, detergent, bread, cheese and whatever grocery items he thinks will sell. I nervously enter and buy three brown bread rolls and a block of cheese. Lunch. We sit near the church and eat slowly. The apartment block opposite is being given a fresh coat of paint. Guess what colour?

Food and the colour yellow works its magic. It's as if a switch has been flicked on our day. The mist lifts and the scenery expands to freshly ploughed fields and pristine forests. The next village, Zdarek is lovely. All the houses look freshly painted and have well-tended gardens. The simple white church is reflected in a clear pond. There's no traffic save for a tractor driven by an angular old man in a beige cap and green overalls. We crest a hill and come upon my favourite Eastern European Image. The village with an incomprehensible name.

Welcome to Tis u Blatna. Six hundred metres above sea level, with a population nudging one hundred, Tis u Blatna has a simple white-painted church with yellow buttresses and a number of plain dwellings for sale. I imagine a cunning real estate agent has convinced the owners to offer their outbuildings for sale. Some look little bigger than sheds and aviaries. I wonder how the sales pitch goes?

Rural living at its finest.

Easy to maintain open plan dwelling with garden views.

A blank canvas for the artistic buyer.

Smell the countryside.

Outside of Tis u Blatna, the road is lined with wild apple trees, groaning with fruit.

Pick fruit from your very own orchard!

I park Craig under a tree and pick an apple. It's tart and juicy and much better than I expected from such an old tree. I'm surprised the locals don't pick them for apple pie. Apple jelly. Apple juice. Apple strudel.

Start your own business in this rural slice of heaven.

We resist the temptations of my inner real estate agent and continue on to Jesenice, our destination for the evening. The centre of town has two closed restaurants, an ice cream shop and a gossip of old ladies in head scarves and black dresses. Our hotel is located on the outskirts of town. We trundle along a bumpy path following the signs and eventually come to a modern building on a rise above a lake. I walk into the foyer and can't resist ringing the bell on the counter a few times. A man immediately rushes through the office door. We don't share a common language but he seems to understand what we want, leading us up to our first floor room. Although the hotel overlooks a sizeable lake, it's designed in such a way that most rooms don't have a view. If I lean out of our side window, I can just see a corner of the lake. We do however have an expansive view of the empty car park.

We wander the grounds. A huge bramble bush runs the length of the rear garden so it's impossible to access the water. There's a newly laid tennis court, an empty swimming pool, an undercover eating area and three concrete bungalows that surely existed before the hotel was built. Bugs attracted by the scent of human flesh drive us back to the restaurant where a portly lady makes Cathie a waffle with ice-cream and fruit. I settle on a beer. And a bite of Cathie's delicious waffle. And a few bites of Cathie's ... oh okay, we share the waffle.

At dinner, we are the only guests. I eat Moravian Pork, a variation on goulash. Cathie makes do with a simple grilled chicken and salad.

She obviously ate too much waffle.

In the middle of the night, I hear a strange noise and go to investigate. I can't find anything unusual, except a gate has been locked on the stairs leading to our floor. It means if there's a fire, we'll have to jump out the window. When I return to bed, I warn Cathie. She tells me to go to sleep. So much for unselfish heroism.

In the morning, the breakfast buffet is artfully arranged just for us. The hotel has thirty-two rooms and only one was filled last night. The staff are unflinchingly kind and attentive. When I ask for plain yoghurt instead of flavoured, the young woman retreats to the kitchen and returns with a large bowlful. I forgive them last night's confinement.

It's drizzling rain this morning as we set off, back down the bumpy path. Jesenice is still asleep. A gold-tinged statue of Jesus hangs from a cross opposite the supermarket. At nearby Orácov, we're greeted with a stone statue of the Virgin Mary watching our progress from under a tree, a pile of glistening orange leaves at her feet. I check my Garmin. We've cycled six kilometres and yet I've rarely pedalled. I do love a downhill in the drizzle. Even Craig seems content. The road closes in under a yellow forest, a train track shadows us. I wonder if it's still in use? Psovlky offers a stone priest, his staff held by his side, looking suitably serious in the fine rain. A woman in purple track pants, her dark hair tied in a ponytail smiles and says hello as we pass. She's pulling weeds in the garden and looks happy to be engaging in physical labour while the rest of the village sleeps.

After seventeen kilometres of beatific cycling, averaging well above our usual speed, ignoring the steady rain and admiring the autumn beauty of the landscape, I turn to Cathie and say, 'Are these the easiest kilometres of our journey?'

She smiles in answer.

Then Craig gets a puncture. I kid you not. From memory, this is his eighth puncture of the trip. Jenny still hasn't had one.

I'm so blissfully happy with this morning's ride that I don't swear. I casually remove the panniers, release the brake cable and calmly turn Craig upside down in the mud of a newly ploughed field. This gives me great pleasure. His handlebars and seat sink into the soil. I repair the tube. It has four patches in it already. I show them to Craig, counting them off in a deliberate voice. Craig sinks further into the soil. I replace the wheel on Craig and we ride silently into Rakovník, hoping for a bike shop. Time for a new tube.

Rakovník is an industrial town with a line of supermarkets on the outskirts. None sell bike tubes. In the town centre the square is crowded with tents and stalls for an open-air market. The pink and white town hall resembles a decorative cake. The elegant church tolls its bells from one end of the square. There is a bike shop around the corner. I buy two tubes. The owner takes Craig out the back to pump up his tyres and returns to explain through mime that my ugly red bicycle needs new ball bearings on the front wheel. I sigh. Craig always needs something. The mechanic wobbles Craig's wheel to convince me of the urgency of the situation. I nod and promise to return in thirty minutes. There's only one thing to do. Eat cake.

Back in the main square, a tavern looks like the only chance of coffee. The owner is a friendly chap who speaks limited English and makes excellent coffee. The cakes are superb - rich layers of cream and nuts, I repeat 'velmi dobrý' over and over. I trust I'm pronouncing 'very good' correctly. He smiles in appreciation.

Craig is wheeled from the back room by the owner who has run the business for twenty years. He takes a map out from under the counter and shows me the best route to Beroun, explaining with elaborate hand movements that we have some hills to traverse. The repair bill for Craig is very cheap, but still more than my bicycle deserves.

A few hundred metres out of town we join bicycle path #303 and ride alongside a lovely river. Yet again, there is barely any need to pedal. The bitumen path leads us through golden tunnels of autumn leaves. I stop frequently to take photographs of Cathie and Jenny. Craig lies in the grass, out of the frame. He has some work to do to regain my affection.

The path only gets better, if that's possible. We cross numerous narrow wooden bridges and glide through a tunnel of trees. Our tyres are caressed by a feather-bed of fallen leaves. We've entered hobbit land. After another bridge, we cross a wide field surrounded by golden forest. I'm half-expecting to see a bear lumbering through the undergrowth, it's so magical.

At Městecko we rejoin the mountain road and cruise down hill to Krivoklát where a 12th century castle keeps its secrets on a rocky outcrop. The castle has been a royal house and a prison, before recently becoming a museum. The village spreads out around its base. There's a restaurant next to the Hotel Sykora with heavy wooden outdoor tables and chairs. It's painted bright yellow and looks very welcoming. I order a burger and chips and Cathie her usual goats cheese salad. Hardly Czech food, but it is delicious and washed down with cheap Pilsener. What more could we ask?

When I return to Craig, I tell him I'm considering donating him to the ugliest meanest man with the largest dog I can find in the Czech Republic. He'll spend his days cowering in the corner of a shed full of motorbikes and Rottweiler puppies who piss on his wheels. He remains mute. Cathie suppresses a smile. She knows I'd never part with my unfaithful companion.

A few kilometres on at Roztoky, the road turns away from the river and rises into the forest. The climbing begins. It's magnificent. At regular intervals we look up into the overhanging forest and see little brown timber cottages clinging to the sides of the hill. They are no bigger than a single room with a jaunty verandah at the front. Cubby houses for grown-ups. Around the next corner, someone has drawn a mouse face on an upturned log, using found objects for its eyes and nose. The mouse is smiling and so are we. The road rises for a marvellous five kilometres, barely changing from its 4% gradient. The perfect hill climb.

At the summit, we have 360 degree views across the distant hills. We've gained the high ground and for the next hour cruise along a perfect tarmac past rolling fields and stone villages. A few kilometres from our destination we have a choice of roads. Downhill on our present course or along a narrow path through yet one more hilltop forest. It's been such a perfect day, we can't resist. The path takes us along a precipice looking down on the villages of Stradonice and Hyskov, before a winding descent to the Pension Bartak located on a hill just outside of Beroun.

The owner greets us warmly and promises to take care of our bikes while we inspect our room on the first floor. It's homely and clean and very cheap. We walk into town and eat a delicious cake with coffee in a small cafe near the zentrum. Most people are heading home from work but, disconcertingly, a few seem to be quite drunk. A man staggers from a bar, dressed in a bright red and green sports outfit, earplugs in, singing loudly. He spies a pretty girl working in a grocery store and tries to figure out what to buy just so he can talk to her. He can't decide between a chocolate bar and a slushy. She smiles indulgently. Outside a fashion store twenty metres away, a man lies prostrate on the ground, an empty bottle in his outstretched hand. People walk past and stare.

Further on, another man wanders across the footpath smiling to himself, his legs wobbly, his hands trying to scratch his beard but poking himself in the eye instead. I wonder if there's a prolonged happy hour that causes such public drunkenness?

Back at the pension, I search the internet for famous people from Beroun. Disconcertingly, the first name that comes up is Monica Sweetheart, a porn star. The second most famous person linked to Beroun according to cyberspace is Vaclav Talich, a classical music conductor born in Moravia who died here in 1961. From an artist to a porn star. Does this symbolise the diminution of culture in the past half century? The photos of Vaclav show a darkly handsome man with a broad forehead and a downturned mouth. He's dressed in a pinstripe suit. The photos of Ms Sweetheart show a lot of cleavage.

The restaurant attached to our pension features the owner as chef and his wife as the waitress. We both order beef soup with Celestine noodles, a hearty dish, followed by Hungarian chicken, hot and spicy, perhaps inspired by Ms Sweetheart? Yet again, the bill is very cheap.

Chapter Seventeen:

Bohemia, Czech Republic

The owner surprises us by delivering breakfast to our room. So we enjoy the guilt-free indulgence of two perfectly cooked eggs with ham and cheese, bread, juice and coffee.

Before leaving the hotel room, I kiss Cathie once more. Today is our final day on the road. I want to tell her how much I love her and appreciate her serene presence on this trip. Without her, Craig would have ended up in the bottom of a river. She smiles and tells me we still have to make it to Prague today.

Perhaps Cathie knew something I didn't. Craig greets me in the shed with yet another flat tyre. I can't believe it. Worse still, when I'm changing the tube, I notice a number of tiny cracks in the rim. He's collapsing before my eyes from too many cobblestones and rough tracks. I'm not sure whether to feel sorry for him or use it as an excuse to buy a new bike. I do neither, instead cruising downhill to the only bike shop in town. It's closed. We wait thirty minutes for it to open before the owner tells me they don't have a suitable wheel. It's looks like Craig's going to have to struggle through the pain and deliver me to Prague in his present arthritic condition. Or not?

We cycle alongside the fast flowing Berounka river on a lonely backroad. It traces a narrow gorge with steep cliffs on one side and a train track on the other. I wince every time we shudder over the cobblestones of each small village. After not worrying for two thousand five hundred kilometres, now in the final fifty, every bump could mean the end of the journey. In normal circumstances I'd battle up the two kilometre hill to look at Karlstjin Castle, but with Craig in convalescence, we make do with coffee and pancakes at the riverside village.

Near Cerenice, we join cycle route #3 which promises to lead us directly into the centre of Prague and our self-appointed finish line - the Charles Bridge. It's a lovely path for ten kilometres following the glistening river. We're blessed with a cloudless sky and temperature in the mid twenties. It's hard to believe it's October.

When we're seven kilometres from Prague and can almost smell the finish, the track diverts away from the river and we're tossed amongst the city traffic. We wobble between the kerb and tram tracks.

Cathie is followed up hill by a very patient tram driver.

I've had enough. At the next traffic light I turn right and head towards the river. Luckily, this takes us to a bike lane on a busy road. After so long in the countryside, it's weird to be surrounded by so many people. I don't think they're here to celebrate our arrival.

In the distance, I can see Charles Bridge. The Dancing House. And St Vitus Cathedral on the hill. The Prague Castle. We have arrived! Almost.

It's lunch time. Given our focus on food throughout this jaunt, we decide it's fitting to eat lunch at a riverside cafe before our spiritual finish on the bridge. It's a lovely day and the citizens of Prague are eating in outdoor cafes, on bench seats in parks and strolling along with a sandwich beside the Vltava river.

At a sunny cafe we eat delicious plates of risotto. It's not Czech food, but we plan to indulge tonight and in the following few days of our stay in this regal capital of Bohemia. The friendly waitress asks where we've cycled from and is astonished by the reply. She's a proud Prague native and implores us to stay in her city for as long as possible. We assure her we will.

And so onto Charles Bridge among the heaving crowds of snap happy tourists. We ask a young woman to take our photo under the Statue of the Saints and instead of holding hands, we hug our bicycles. It's because of Craig and Jenny that we've made it this far. I forgive Craig his sins and once again applaud Jenny and my beautiful wife for their achievements.

Decorated with thirty statues, the 14th century bridge is one of the most photographed structures in the Czech Republic. Lined with stalls of local artists selling jewellery and paintings and despite all the statues being replicas, it still maintains an aura of Gothic splendour. My favourite bridge in the world, mercifully free of cars. A crowd lines up in front of the Statue of St John Nepomuk. It's considered good luck to touch the plinth. Not that it helped the original St John who was tossed from this bridge in 1393 by order of King Wenceslaus, the ruler of Bohemia.

We cycle slowly through the old town, stopping near the famous Astrological Clock, surely the most overrated tourist sight in Prague. Underwhelming is an overstatement. I prefer the ornate beauty of the Opera House, the cubist simplicity of the Orient Cafe, the humour and irreverence of the Dancing House and the Gothic majesty of St Vitus Cathedral. But still, people line up to photograph the clock on the hour, every hour. It's the oldest functioning astrological clock and there is some humour in the four figures of ridicule - vanity, greed, death and entertainment. Not sure about the last one, but it was installed six centuries ago when fun perhaps wasn't high on everyone's pious agenda.

We locate our apartment along a cobblestone street in the Jewish quarter. Predictably, a beautiful young woman named Nicol greets us and shows us to our apartment. It's huge. I can't believe we're in the centre of Prague and paying less for this luxury than we would for a dumpy one-star motel in a mid-size Australian town. Nicol sets about ringing bicycle shops to locate a proper size wheel to fit everyone's favourite troublemaker, Craig.

We spend our afternoon in bicycle surgery. Craig pulls through and we celebrate by locking him and his sparkling new wheel behind a solid wooden double door while Cathie and I return to the old town in search of dinner. Our celebration meal.

The Casserol restaurant is located in a 12th century cellar. We're lead past the open kitchen where the chefs all look up from their stations to say hello. It's a disarming habit. My piglet knuckle and Cathie's duck are pretty damn impressive as well. As is the beer. We've ridden precisely two thousand five hundred and fifteen kilometres to quench our thirst.

After dinner we wander the alleyways of the old town. Prague rivals Paris as a city of romance with Gothic buildings, narrow cobblestone streets and outdoor cafes opening onto historic squares. We hold hands and play silly games like trying to pick our favourite day, our best meal, the section we'd most like to cycle again. There are so many, it's impossible to choose. We've been blessed with good weather, fine food, bucket loads of beer and a path that winds through some of Europe's best scenery and most important towns. The Euro Velo 4 is less well-known than the Euro Velo 6, but I consider it the equal of its more famous sister route.

Long may it prosper.

Chapter Eighteen:

Prague, Czech Republic

We're so used to waking early it's become automatic. The apartment doesn't offer breakfast. I'm eager to walk the quiet streets before the thousands of fellow tourists clog every artery of the old town. We quickly get dressed into normal clothes - bye bye lycra - and walk through the deserted streets. Without people, the Art Nouveau buildings have space to impose their unique character, free from hawkers, tourists and advertising signs. It's magic. There's just Cathie and me and the street sweepers. On the Charles Bridge, we're joined by a newly married couple still awake from last night's celebrations. She's carrying her wedding dress, he's still smart in a tuxedo. I hope it's been a memorable first night of many for them. We stand at the entry to the bridge and look down the avenue of statues. The early morning sunlight glints off the cobblestones, a lone cyclist pedals towards us and the wedding couple link arms under the statue of St John. We lean over the bridge. A lone fisherman in a wooden dinghy hauls a large fish into his net. I feel like applauding.

On the left bank down an alleyway is Cukr Kava Limonada, a corner cafe that offers home made pastries and excellent scrambled eggs and coffee. The place quickly fills with hipsters and we both feel like wayward grandparents let loose from the old people's home. We take our decrepit bodies up the hill to St Vitus Cathedral, a brooding Gothic masterpiece hemmed in by lesser buildings on all sides. Inside the Cathedral is a mesmerising banquet of brightly-coloured stain-glass windows, silver angels holding drapes over a gold-embossed casket, numerous crypts housing the remains of Bohemian kings and enough snarling lions and ancient paintings to fill a museum. It's so over the top, I'm not sure where to look next. I settle on the chapel of St Wenceslaus, the patron saint of the Czech State. Anybody who has a Christmas hymn written about them can't be all bad. His chapel takes pride of place in the cathedral he founded on this spot in 930.

After all this dazzle, it's pleasant to stroll in the so-called 'Golden Alley,' a narrow lane of very small houses that contain recreations of the lives of everyday workers throughout the history of Prague. The Herbalist house is entered past a toilet alcove. I wonder how a herbalist could work with the breeze blowing past the toilet into his small office.

They obviously didn't study feng shui in the 11th century.

We wander back to the old town, across the human traffic jam of the Charles Bridge. So many hawkers, so many iPhone selfies, so much crush. It's a relief to find Cafe Cafe. What is it about Prague and silly cafe names? It's a cool comfortable room with elegant light fittings, handsome waiters and a very pretentious clientele.

Overheard at the next table. One hipster says to his friend, 'So, I'm on stage in one room reading love letters to Jessica and she's in another room reading love letters to me.' At another table, a middle-aged woman talks about publishing her first book. Doesn't anyone have a normal profession anymore? Where are the storemen, accountants, bank clerks? Working, I imagine. Not hanging out for hours in a Prague cafe like we are.

Cafe Cafe offers modern Czech food. The ingredients are fresh and well prepared. Bring your earplugs.

In the late afternoon, we walk to Wenceslaus Square, scene of the Velvet Revolution. The square is traffic-clogged and reverberates to the sound of hip hop. McDonalds and Burger King have replaced raised fists and megaphones shouting for liberty. Freedom has arrived and it offers happy meals for two hundred korunas.

Prague has perhaps the most beautiful people in Europe - women with high cheekbones and long legs; gaunt men born to be artists wear corduroy trousers, scruffy beards and serious expressions. It's enough to make an old poet wish he was young again.

We wander this Art Nouveau and Cubist wonderland, our heads tilted upwards as if in search of the answer to history's logic through architecture. At least the tops of these majestic buildings are largely free of advertising. It's time for another chimney cake.

When we arrive back at our apartment late in the evening, I walk across to where Craig and Jenny wait, ready for our next adventure. I touch their handlebars, pat their seats and check the tyre pressure before wishing them good night. In a few days we leave Prague, by train. Craig and Jenny have earned a long and welcome rest.

Until our next adventure.

15599637R00076

Printed in Great Britain
by Amazon